LEXICON OF
ROCK GARDENS

A guide for successful construction and planting

Hermann Hackstein &
Wota Wehmeyer

REBO
PUBLISHERS

© 2005 Rebo International b.v., Lisse, The Netherlands
1st edition 2006 Rebo Publishers

Author: Herman Hackentein & Wota Wehmeyer
Typesetting: AdAm Studio, Prague, The Czech Republic
Translator: Patricia Cooke for First Edition Translations Ltd,
Cambridge, UK
Editor: Sally Heavens for First Edition Translations Ltd
Proofreading: Sarah Dunham

ISBN 90 366 1890 8

Contents

Using natural stone

THE FASCINATION OF NATURAL STONE

The urge to discover and explore other lands, other continents, has over the centuries driven men and women out into the world. These men and women risked their lives for the undertaking.

Extreme terrain seems to exert the greatest attraction. Tropical rain forests and arctic ice, deserts, semi-deserts, and high mountain regions continue to cast their spells on adventurers and explorers to this day.

The travel writings of great naturalists such as Maria Sybilla Merian, Johann Wolfgang von Goethe, Alexander von Humboldt, Sven Hedin, and others, together with accounts from the European colonies, kindled widespread interest in the exotic and unusual and the desire to recreate these experiences at home. Thus, alongside zoological gardens, botanical gardens, and natural history museums, increasing numbers of private gardens came into being—their allure remains as strong as ever today.

There are many possibilities for rock garden enthusiasts wishing to introduce plants from the barren high mountain zones of Europe and Asia or the arid regions of North America, South Africa, and Australia into their own gardens, bringing distant regions to their doorsteps and capturing a world in microcosm.

A BONUS FOR THE GARDEN

Every garden improves with the studied inclusion of rocks or stones as a visual element. The spectrum of possible formations is enormous, ranging from a solitary boulder that draws the eye to complete rock gardens. This is not all, however: incorporating rocks adds dimension for the gardener. Many plants find their ideal living conditions between stones; from inconspicuous thyme, clinging closely to stone surfaces, to filigree soapwort, the beauty of which is only disclosed on closer inspection, to luxuriant aubrietia, commanding attention in spring with its exuberant mass of flowers.

Added to these are the innumerable plants that are best displayed to full effect in combination with natural stone: trees such as dwarf pine and Japanese maple, tall specimens like mullein or sunflowers, and smaller flowers such as candelabra primulas and asters.

Incorporating rocks into the garden is so much more than mere decoration: it offers a unique opportunity to experience a fascinating facet of nature and to enjoy it outside your door.

USEFUL AIDS

Stone in the garden has a practical function over and above the visual component: it can be used to good effect from the basic layout of a garden to its detailed final design.

There are a variety of uses, including reinforcing slopes with large blocks of stone and dry stone walls; defining different areas of the garden; edging low beds or paths with small stones; providing stepping stones in larger beds; and furnishing large-scale paved paths and terraces.

Ultimately, a garden design without stone is barely conceivable, though the visual importance accorded this natural material will of course vary according to individual requirements and taste.

Shapes and variants

No two rock gardens are the same—and not just because of the great variety of constructional styles. Quite simply, every rock is unique. Each one has its own individual shape and charisma. Thus, a natural boulder differs from a rough-hewn quarry stone as much as it does from an industrially processed, reconstructed stone.

To this must be added the inexhaustible variety of materials. From dark porphyry, red sandstone, to sandy travertine—there is hardly a color in nature that cannot be found in natural stone. In addition, the color changes according to weather conditions—the dull, matte surface of a dry rock will gleam after a shower of rain.

Each stone, too, presents a different structure; the prominent veining of many marbles, coarse-grained granite, the uni-

form surface of limestone. The unique appearance of natural stone is further enriched by its form, whether brittle layers of slate, the irregular shape of a quarry stone, or smooth, patio paving.

Rockery beds

CREATING A BEAUTIFUL FLOWERBED WITH STONE

A rock garden consists of rocks incorporated attractively and lovingly into the planting areas. In nature, rock plants find their habitats among naturally occurring rubble and stones, while in the garden rocks must be carefully arranged so that the plants can enjoy optimal growing conditions.

When constructing beds from natural stone there are two basic alternatives: either combine several stones to form an assemblage or deliberately use larger rocks as focal points within the flowerbed. Isolated rocks used in this way are known as "accents".

GROUPS OF ROCKS

The only way to create the impression of a "genuine" rock garden is to introduce several rocks into the planting area. The visual effect naturally depends, not only on the number and size of

the rocks used, but also—and to a greater extent—on their overall arrangement and color combination. An attractive rock garden will not result from randomly depositing a couple of stones on a flowerbed.

Natural effect

The simplest construction is a rocky mound. The largest rocks are placed in the middle with smaller ones around the edges or on top.

So that the rock plants will have sufficient nutrients to grow, it is important to fill the crevices and spaces between rocks with soil. It is best to use ready-made compost, as this is very fine and loose. Introduce the compost by allowing it to trickle into the cracks, pressing it in place as firmly as you can with your hands. Then settle it in by watering. The compost will sink, whereupon more compost should be pressed into the cracks. If you are constructing a larger rocky mound it is important to introduce the soil gradually between all the layers of rock and not just fill any visible cracks at the edges. Only by filling all crevices with soil will you give your rock plants the optimal opportunity to take root and become established.

FORMAL DESIGN

Emulating nature is, however, only one of many design possibilities. It can be equally attractive to integrate stones into the planting areas according to formal principles.

Thus, for example, a Japanese garden achieves an exciting contrast using raked gravel surfaces and single trees positioned as focal points. And planting areas covered with light-colored pebbles go particularly well with modern architecture.

Single rocks as focal points

In nature only a few large rocks stand out from their surroundings sufficiently to catch the eye. But your own garden offers the opportunity to position particularly beautiful examples directly in the field of view.

Whether or not such solitary rocks are aesthetically pleasing depends to a great extent on the planting around them. Ideally,

no soil should be visible—dense ground-cover plants or small stones are particularly good for this purpose.

The more clearly the rock stands out from its surroundings, the more dramatic the effect will be. Solitary rocks should therefore be positioned against a backdrop that is as evenly hued as possible and that forms a clear contrast to the color of the stone.

Particularly suitable are plants of medium height with dense green foliage and an unobtrusive leaf structure. Evergreens are best. Their height should also be in sympathy with the size of the rock.

WALLS AND SUPPORTS

For centuries, man has used rock to reinforce soil and to build walls. So it seems entirely appropriate to use natural stone in the garden to retain soil or to define areas, whether as a low edging for beds, as medium-sized supporting walls, or for reinforcing massive slopes.

The possibilities are endless, not only from the point of view of height and stability, but also, and more especially, in terms of form and technical execution.

DRY-STONE WALLS

Dry-stone walls are one of the most popular uses of stone in the garden. They are built from small, rough-hewn blocks of stone. There are two ways to build dry-stone walls: fairly low walls which will not be exposed to any great static loading can be built simply by layering stones on top of each other. Larger walls or walls that have to retain heavy soil on slopes must be constructed in rigid form, using mortar.

Building walls without mortar offers the opportunity to fill the gaps with soil, thus creating favorable living conditions for plants. But a wall built with mortar does not need to be bare and monotonous—particularly if it is retaining soil. In this case, ground-cover plants and carpets of flowers can trail over the wall, to picturesque and romantic effect.

When building smallish walls up to a height of around 20 in (0.5 m) it is generally sufficient to consolidate the ground before laying the stones. Larger walls, on the other hand, need a stable foundation. They are best built on a bed of crushed rock.

It is quite possible to build smaller dry-stone walls yourself. It is simply a matter of selecting suitably shaped stones and placing them carefully. The wall should not slope outwards, but should always have a slight incline toward the bed or the slope of the ground.

WALLS MADE FROM RECONSTRUCTED STONE

No less attractive are walls made from hewn or industrially processed, reconstructed stone. They produce a clear, simple style that is particularly suited to modern or formal gardens. These walls are built with mortar and are generally unsuitable for planting.

It is possible, however, to mitigate their somewhat severe appearance with overhanging flowers or easy growing rock plants at their base.

Slope reinforcement

There are two ways of reinforcing steep slopes: either terrace the slope and build several small walls, or reinforce it with stable breast walls made from large blocks of stone. This work must, of course, be left to specialists.

EDGINGS

While large walls are mainly recommended in sloping situations, shallow edgings can be incorporated into any garden design. Natural stone can be used to provide a stylish edge for beds or an attractive border for paths and terraces.

With edgings, too, there is a choice between natural stone, mainly irregular in size and shape, and reconstructed stone of various types. Careful matching of these to the terrace or path materials will create a particularly harmonious effect. Where bed edgings are concerned, however, a lot depends on whether they are intended simply as inconspicuous, functional markers for the edge of the bed, or as more prominent design features.

Basically, edgings mark off planting areas from other parts of the garden—e.g., the lawn—and contain the flowers within their bed. They can also be used to separate larger areas within the garden and, in this way, can underscore the division of a garden into various visual "zones".

WATER & ROCK

Rock gardens gain special value through the introduction of water. This natural element energizes the deadweight of stone—whether lapping gently round pebbles at the edge of a pond, babbling inquisitively over the bed of a stream, or splashing soothingly out of a rocky fountain, water in the garden holds endless fascination for both the ear and the eye.

The best type of stream for a rock garden is one in which the bed is constructed from natural stones of different sizes. Sloping positions are especially suitable, as they create the possibility for small waterfalls. Even on level sites, however, skillful positioning of the stones enables the construction of numerous streams that flow pleasingly into one small pond. From there the water can be pumped back to the beginning of the watercourses. Rocky zones, going far beyond the function of stream boundary, can also be constructed around the pond itself.

PATHS & TERRACES

Last but not least, natural stone is also eminently suitable for laying paths and terraces. These pedestrian surfaces, when made from natural material, are also particularly well suited to a rock garden.

Large slabs of natural stone are the first choice for constructing fairly large, paved surfaces. They can either be laid closely, abutting one another, or arranged some distance apart. The spaces between can then be filled either with gravel or grass. This has the effect of breaking up large surfaces and creating a more natural appearance. Irregularly broken slabs are perfectly suited for this purpose.

Broken slabs also make the best type of stepping stone for plant beds. Laying paths in this way is not only more economical than paving, but also less obtrusive, with the stones blending into the backdrop of the rock plants.

Another possibility is to use hewn stone blocks, which are available in all paving stone sizes. Two-inch square (5 cm x 5 cm) and four-inch square (10 cm x 10 cm) blocks are very popular for paths and terraces, as are four by two-inches rectangular

(10 cm x 5 cm) ones. Granite in particular is inexpensive and can be hewn to a very high quality.

Cut stone of this kind is also available in considerably larger sizes, which can be used, not only for constructing dry-stone walls, but also for building stairs. The stones can either be placed close together, to form a fairly steep stairway, or wider apart, to form steps with gravel in between.

The overall effect of the rock garden will be especially harmonious if the natural materials used coordinate with each other. This impression is easily achieved by using particular types of rock in different places. Thus, for example, reconstructed granite can be used to pave paths and surfaces, while uncut stones can be used in the beds.

A–Z of plants

Individual taste

Of course, it is not only the rocks, whether incorporated as functional or aesthetic elements, which determine the successful design of a rock garden. The plants are inextricably linked with them—and it is the plants that bring the rock garden to life.

There are a number of rock plants that require little soil or attention to thrive. They are, however, mostly very low growing and relatively inconspicuous. They do  have their place in the rock garden, but the overall effect will be determined by larger or more striking plants. These include shrubs and ferns as well as perennials and annuals. But, as noted earlier, the choice of plants is first and foremost a question of individual taste, so it is perfectly possible, for example, to integrate useful plants such as herbs or fruit bushes into the rock garden as well.

THE PLANT PORTRAITS

There are, however, a large number of plants that are usually associated with rock gardens. In the following pages, over 130 plant portraits cover the most important of these.

Such a selection can make no claim to completeness and by its very nature is subjective, reflecting the preferences of the editors. In some cases, the portraits present in greater detail certain sub-species that are particularly popular and suitable for rock gardens.

THE INFORMATION BOXES

In order to make it a little easier for you to choose plants for your own garden, a small information box has been included in each plant portrait.

5 - 10 cm

VI-VIII

The first line indicates the preferred position, with the top symbols showing whether the plant prefers full sun, partial shade, or total shade.

The second line shows the height of the fully-grown plant. This can vary greatly according to species. In several portraits, this information refers to the most common varieties of the plant; indications as to which species grow taller or shorter can be found in the text.

Finally, the flowering time, where applicable, is given in months (Roman numerals beside a flower symbol).

Abies balsamea

BALSAM FIR

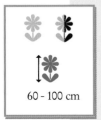

60 - 100 cm

The firs (*Abies*) belong to the Pine family (*Pinaceae*) and occur as various species in the northern hemisphere. *Abies balsamea*, also known as Balsam Fir, originally comes from North America.

The dwarf varieties are of particular interest for the rock garden, where they contribute a valuable structural element. Their special attraction lies in the various forms of growth and range of needle colors and shapes.

One very pretty example is the Dwarf Balsam Fir (*Abies balsamea*, "Nana").

In contrast to its larger relatives, which can attain heights of up to 50 ft (15 m), its maximum height is 24–40 in (60–100 cm). In addition, it grows extremely slowly, only reaching a height of about 24 in (60 cm) after 10 years. Its spherical, cushion-like growth and short, dark-green needles produce a very attractive effect.

The plant prefers a sunny to partially shaded position and grows well in fresh, nutrient-rich soils. It is sensitive to excessively dry conditions. The Dwarf Balsam Fir is also suitable for planting in troughs.

Acaena

New Zealand Burr

5 - 10 cm

✱ VI-VIII

The New Zealand Burr is a representative of the Rose family (*Rosaceae*) and is native to South America and New Zealand. It is an excellent ground-cover plant with a variety of uses. Its rapid growth makes it a good gap-filler. You must be prepared, however, to take remedial action from time to time as it can overwhelm weaker neighbors.

This evergreen plant forms an attractive carpet with its green to blue-gray to bronze pinnate leaves. It has inconspicuous flowers, but from July onward these turn into spectacular, spiny seed heads. New Zealand burrs thrive in full sun, but will also do well in shadier parts of the rock garden. They look particularly attractive among blue- and red-hued grasses and shrubs.

Popular species:

- ACAENA BUCHANANII: a dwarf, silvery-gray plant with green or yellow burrs, which grows to a height of just two inches (5 cm).

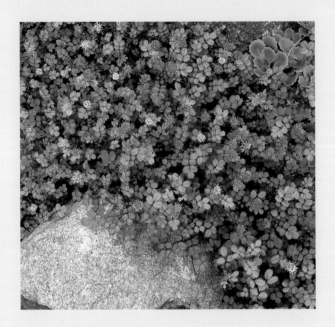

■ ACAENA CAESIIGLAUCA: this vigorous plant forms a blue-gray carpet. It is rather invasive, however, and therefore only recommended for larger areas.

■ ACAENA MICROPHYLLA: this variety, with brownish-green leaves, is more restrained in its growth, but still gives good ground cover. The ornamental variety *Kupferteppich* ("copper carpet") has attractive, bronze foliage and bright red burrs. Its less exuberant growth makes it suitable for smaller rock gardens.

Acer

Maple

100 - 300 cm

IV-V

The maples (*Acer*) belong to the Maple family (*Aceraceae*). Some of the trees or shrubs are native to Europe, while others come from America or Asia. The botanical name *Acer* comes from the Latin and means "sharp" or "pointed", undoubtedly a reference to the shape of the maple leaf.

When laying out a rock garden, shrubs and trees are used to give the basic outline and to provide a framework of plants. Careful thought should be given to their position, as they are mostly very long-lived.

The ornamental value of trees and shrubs lies not only in their different, decorative forms of growth, as in *Acer ginnala* (right), but also in their foliage, which can be quite stunning, especially in the species with colored leaves or attractive fall tints.

It is not surprising, therefore, that the many species of maple are very popular—their main attractions being their beautiful crowns and foliage. The maple is deciduous: in fall the color palette of the leaves ranges from glowing gold, warm orange to intense red. Two maple species especially popular in the rock garden are *Acer japonicum* and *Acer palmatum*.

Popular species:

■ ACER PALMATUM: this is the common, Smooth Japanese Maple, "with leaves like an open hand". It has spreading growth and reaches a height of 40–120 in (100–300 cm). This species of Japanese Maple prefers partial shade and humus-rich soil.

Red-leaved maples are especially popular in the rock garden; these species have the additional name "atropurpureum". A number of maples also have finely cut leaves, a feature indicated by "dissectum" in the name.

Especially recommended is *Acer palmatum atropurpureum* (left), also known as Red or Purple Japanese Maple: it has dark red-purple leaves in summer that turn to gleaming

carmine red in fall. Equally popular are the "Dissectum Atropurpureum Group", also known as Cutleaf Japanese Maples, which have striking, finely cut, red-purple leaves.

— ACER JAPONICUM (right): this species, also known as Downy Japanese Maple, is a low-growing bush of about 48–100 in (120–250 cm) in the variety known as Golden Moon Maple "Aureum". It has very spreading growth, with pink to dark-red flowers that appear between April and May. The plant prefers a light, humus-rich soil that can be slightly acid, and thrives best in partial shade.

Achillea

Yarrow

Yarrows (left) belong to the Composite or Aster family (*Asteraceae*). The Common Yarrow (*Achillea millefolium*) has long been known as a medicinal plant for its anti-inflammatory, antiseptic, and blood-stanching properties. According to legend, it was also used as a medicinal herb by the Greek hero, Achilles, during the Trojan War, giving rise to its botanical name of "Achillea".

There are a number of different species of yarrow. Thus, for example, there are small, silver-gray, white-flowered plants; vigorous, golden-yellow border plants; red-flowered plants; evergreen and herbaceous species; and spring-, summer-, and perpetual-flowering kinds. One example of a white-flowered yarrow is *Achillea ptarmica* (top right), also known as Sneezewort.

In the rock garden this species prefers a sunny position and well-drained soil. Several varieties of

20 - 70 cm

✳ IV-IX

Achillea ptarmica are available. Besides "Major", "The Pearl", and "Nana Compacta", "Schneeball" is particularly attractive. This flowers for several months from about June through September, and grows to a height of 10–28 in (25–70 cm). Its brilliant white, spherical flowers are reminiscent of small pompoms or snowballs.

Aconitum

MONKSHOOD

This plant, which belongs to the Buttercup family (*Ranunculaceae*), is known as monkshood from the shape of its flowers, reminiscent of a monk's hood. It occurs in the northern hemisphere and is represented by about 80 different species. The wild species of monkshood, all protected plants, occur in the mountainous regions of Europe, where they are found in mountain forests, on roadsides, the banks of streams, and in damp meadows. Its beauty, however, ensures that monkshood is also popular in gardens as an ornamental plant.

In the rock garden, monkshood is especially suited for use in edges or as background: growing to a height of up to 100 in (250 cm), it is one of the larger rock garden plants. It prefers a robust, loamy, humus-rich soil and a sunny to partially shaded position, where it can remain undisturbed for a long time.

Aconitum napellus (European Monkshood) is especially popular, with its intense

A HISTORY OF POISON

According to Greek myth, monkshood sprang from the drool of Cerberus, the three-headed guard dog brought out of the underworld by Hercules. That a rather unpleasant story should be used to explain the origins of such an outwardly attractive flower probably stems from the fact that it is one of the most poisonous plants in Europe. From antiquity onward, aconitin was one of the poisons most frequently used to commit murder. It was also used by many cultures to poison arrows for hunting.

blue to violet-blue flowers. It grows to a height of about 20–40 in (50–100 cm) and flowers from June through August. Also very attractive is the pale-yellow *Aconitum lamarckii* (Yellow Monkshood), which flowers from July through August, and the yellow-flowered *Aconitum vulparia* (Yellow Wolfbane). Both do particularly well by streams and at the water's edge. The amethyst-blue flowers of *Aconitum wilsonii* appear from August through October.

50 – 250 cm

VII-X

Adiantum pedatum

NORTHERN MAIDENHAIR FERN

20 - 60 cm

Adiantum pedatum, the Northern Maidenhair Fern, belongs to the Maidenhair Fern family (*Adiantaceae*). The botanical name *Adiantum* (Greek "a" expressing a negative, "dianein" meaning "to wet") indicates that drops of water run off the edges of the pinnae, while *pedatum* indicates that the leaves are divided like toes on a foot.

This fern, with an almost tropical feel, is actually winter hardy, but its shoots should be given some protection against late frosts. Its home is North America (including Alaska), East Asia, and the Himalayas. It is not particularly difficult to grow; while it prefers a moist, humus-rich soil, it will also cope with sandy soils.

The Northern Maidenhair Fern has light-green, fan-shaped fronds that take on a beautiful golden yellow coloring in fall. It is seen to best advantage in partially shaded areas of larger rock gardens, and goes well with shade-loving grasses and colorful spring bulbs.

The variety "Aleuticum", also known as "Imbricatum", is a miniature version of *Adiantum pedatum*. In this variety the blue-green fronds only reach a height of 8 in (20 cm). In spite of its daintiness, it is a robust fern, especially suited to small rock gardens.

Aethionema

15 - 30 cm

✻ IV-VII

Stone Cress

Aethionema, also known as Stone Cress, belongs to the Mustard family (Brassicaceae, Cruciferae) and occurs naturally in rocky crevices, on stony mountain slopes, and in the rocky steppes of the Middle East. For this reason, *Aethionema* species are eminently suitable for the rock garden where they can find similar conditions to those they prefer in nature; for example, scattered between cushion plants and rubble or in crevices. They also do well in troughs.

These small, evergreen sub-shrubs grow to a height of 6–12 in (15–30 cm) and have narrow leaflets with a bluish shimmer. These contrast well with the racemes of flowers. Depending on species and variety, these are mostly pink, but can also be red, lilac, or white. The flowering period is between April and July.

Aethionema prefers full sun and thrives best in dry, sandy, calcareous soil. In general the plant is very easy to care for, but it is sensitive to too much moisture and should be protected from the wet during winter, if necessary.

Popular species:

- **AETHIONEMA ARMENUM:** this species flowers from May through June and grows to a height of about 6–8 in (15–20 cm). Popular varieties are the pink-flowered "Warley Rose" and the dark-pink flowered "Warley Ruber".

- **AETHIONEMA GRANDIFLORUM:** the particularly large, pink flowers of this species, which is also known as Persian Stone Cress, can be seen from June through July. The plant attains a height of about 6–12 in (15–30 cm) and has gray-green leaves. This species is also available in the varieties "Warley Rose" and "Warley Ruber".

- **AETHIONEMA IBERIDEUM:** this species has white flowers from June through July and grows to a height of 4–6 in (10–15 cm).

- **AETHIONEMA SCHISTOSUM:** this popular subspecies of Stone Cress has white flowers and reaches a height of about 6 in (15 cm).

Ageratum

Floss Flower

10 - 80 cm

V-X

Ageratum, also known as Floss Flower, is a particularly long-lasting flowering plant whose colorful blooms provide bright and cheerful accents in the rock garden for five to six months of the year.

The plants have a tall, upright or cushion-like appearance and have oval to lanceolate, mid-green leaves. The closely packed clusters of small flowers, which are brush-like tufts, can be enjoyed from May through October. The flowers are bright blue, violet, white, or pink, depending on the species, and can form an unbroken carpet of velvety color. The Floss Flower grows to a height of 4–32 in (10–80 cm).

Ageratum prefers a sunny to partially shaded spot and a light, moist, humus-rich soil. The taller species should be deadheaded to promote the formation of new flowers. The more compact varieties of *Ageratum houstanium* are especially well suited to the rock garden, as they only grow to a height of around 6–8 in (15–20 cm). Popular varieties include the mid-blue "Blue Danube", the pale-blue "Blue Mink", and the white-flowered "Hawaii White".

Alchemilla

Lady's Mantle

20 - 60 cm

✳ VI-VIII

Alchemilla, also known as Lady's Mantle, is a genus of many species in the Rose family (Rosaceae).

The yellowy-green flowers of the plant, which can be seen between June and August, are rather insignificant. In compensation, however, Lady's Mantle has particularly attractive, round, matte-green leaves reminiscent of a cloak or mantle. This, and the plant's medically unproven reputation as a remedy for women's ailments, explains the name by which it is commonly known.

A further characteristic of the plant is that drops of rain or dew remain caught on the leaves and their edges, shimmering like glass beads. Even in dry weather, when no water reaches the plant from outside, the plant itself secretes small drops of water in high air humidity, a process known as guttation. The leaves look as if they are covered in precious crystals. This characteristic probably gave rise to the botanical name *Alchemilla*—in the Middle Ages, alchemists are said to have highly valued these drops of water and used them in their experiments.

Alchemilla prefers a sunny to partially shaded position and well drained, but moist, soil that is rich in nutrients. Two well-known species suitable for the rock garden are:

- ALCHEMILLA MOLLIS: the Latin name of this species (*mollis*) means "soft". It is very suitable as a ground-cover plant and can be used to mark the end of a bed in the rock garden. It can attain a height of 8–24 in (20–60 cm), its yellowy-green flowers appearing between June and July.

- ALCHEMILLA SPLENDENS: the Latin name for this species (*splendens*) means "shining". It also has yellowy-green flowers.

Allium

ONION

The genus *Allium* (*Alliaceae*: the Onion family) is represented by about 280 species spread throughout the world. Its occurrence ranges from lowlands to mountains, and it appears in a variety of forms—there are species that only grow to four inches (10 cm) and others that reach heights of up to 60 inches (1.5 m), such as the Giant Onion (*Allium giganteum*) from the Himalayas. Flower color also varies—there are yellow, pink, blue, purple, and white species.

The yellow-flowered Golden Garlic, *Allium moly* (top) from Eastern Spain and Southern France, is a very popular representative of this genus. This smallish species only grows to 8–18 in (20–45 cm). The rounded bulbs produce yellowy-green leaves reminiscent of tulip leaves. The flower stalks are 6–14 in (15–35 cm) long, and the umbels of bright yellow, star-shaped flowers appear from May through June.

Golden Garlic will grow in any position, in both sun and shade. Shady or partially shaded positions are actually best, as the leaf tips burn easily in full sun. For this reason, Golden Garlic is well suited for underplanting trees and shrubs, where it will naturalize.

Allium christophii (bottom), known as the Star of Persia, is a particularly beautiful species.

GARDENING TIP

Ornamental onions combine very well with other plants. It is possible to enjoy the flowers of the ornamental onion throughout the summer by planting early, mid-season, and late species.

Allium schoenoprasum

CHIVES

20 - 30 cm

V-VIII

Chives are universally known and loved as a culinary herb: freshly picked, they are used in salads, soups, and egg dishes, to name but a few. This plant, however, which is indigenous to almost the whole of Europe, can also claim a place among the ornamental plants of this genus, as from May onward the grass-like clumps bear umbels of exquisite, deep-purple to dark-pink flowers.

Chives are very easy to grow. They prefer a moist, nutrient-rich soil in sun to partial shade. One interesting possibility for growing chives in the rock garden is the construction of an herb spiral. This provides both a valuable habitat for beneficial garden creatures and an attractive focal point.

Decorative chive varieties include "Corsican White", a small, white-flowered variety, and "Forescate", a pink-flowered cultivar growing to ten inches (25 cm).

GARDENING TIP

If you want to use chives in the kitchen, you should forego the globular flowers and remove them as soon as possible, as they sap the plant's strength.

Besides chives, a cross between chives and garlic has recently become available. This hybrid, which grows to about 20 in (50 cm), is not only healthy in soups and salads, but also keeps unwanted pests such as flea beetles and aphids at bay.

Alyssum saxatile

Basket of Gold

The cushion-forming *Alyssum* is one of the most popular
rock garden plants of all. This plant, which is indigenous
to Europe and the Middle East, grows naturally on limestone cliffs; in the garden it thrives equally well on scree
beds and between the stones of a dry wall. Here it forms
attractive cushions of small, gray-green leaves, which are
almost completely obscured by its glowing, yellow blossoms during the flowering period.

These sub-shrubs also present a pleasing aspect outside the flowering period, however, as most of the *Alyssum*
species are evergreen. The plants can be induced to make
bushy growth by pinching out the tips after flowering.

The most well known species of *Alyssum* is *Alyssum
saxatile*, also known as Gold Dust or Basket of Gold. The
intense color of its flowers makes it an important element
in the color palette of many gardens. Suitable companion
plants include Aubrietia, Arabis, and Moss Phlox.

POPULAR VARIETIES:

15 - 40 cm

IV-VI

- CITRINUM: this variety is characterized by pale sulfur- to lemon-yellow flowers.

- COMPACTUM: as the name suggests, this is a compact variety, only growing to a height of about eight inches (20 cm). The flowers are golden yellow.

- PLENUM: this variety features double golden-yellow flowers.

- VARIEGATUM: in this variety the leaves have a yellowy-white edge and the flowers are yellow.

Anemone

10 - 120 cm

III-X

WINDFLOWER

The *Anemone* or Windflower belongs to the Buttercup family (Ranunculaceae). The 100 or so species of the genus occur mainly in the northern hemisphere, mostly in the temperate climatic zones of Asia. They have become popular ornamental plants in Central Europeans gardens, which they adorn with their delicate flowers at various times of the year depending on species and variety.

The name "Anemone" comes from "anemos", the Greek word for "wind." In Greek mythology, Anemona was a nymph at the court of the goddess Flora. When Flora's husband, Zephyr the god of the wind, fell in love with Anemona, the jealous wife turned her into a flower, which has borne the name "Anemone" ever since. The delicate flowers move at the slightest breath of wind.

SYMBOL OF INNOCENCE

These flowers, with their rather fragile appearance, have from time immemorial been the symbol of innocence and trust, of the ephemeral and vulnerable. This appearance is deceptive, however, as anemones are actually quite easy, undemanding plants and therefore perfectly suited to rock gardens.

■ ANEMONE BLANDA (right): *Anemone blanda*, also known as the Grecian Windflower, is a spring-flowering anemone, blooming from

March to April. Flower color differs according to the variety. Examples include "Radar", with bright carmine flowers, "White Splendor", with large, white, very robust flowers, and "Atrocoerulea" with large, blue flowers. The leaves are deeply cut and lie on the soil. The plant grows to about eight inches (20 cm) in height and is classed as a small perennial. It does best in light, sandy, humus-rich soil in a partially shaded position.

▬ ANEMONE JAPONICA: This plant, also known as the Japanese or Fall Anemone, prefers a partially shaded position in damp, humus-rich soil. It flowers between August and October. It is typified by pale flowers on long, stable stalks shining in the late-summer shade. These perennials can grow to 48 in (120 cm). *Anemone japonica* exists in white, silvery-pink, purple, dark-pink, and pinky-red forms, some of which have semi-double flowers. Well-known varieties include the white-flowered "Honorine Jobert" and the purple "Prinz Heinrich".

Antennaria dioica

5 - 15 cm

V-VI

PUSSY TOES

The home of the silver-leaved *Antennaria dioica* lies in the temperate and even arctic zones of the earth. The plant grows naturally on poor grassland, in pine forests, and in scrubland. It prefers poor, sandy soils low in nitrogen and rarely grows on decalcified loam. The common names Pussy Toes or Cat's Foot refer to the soft hairs on the inflorescence.

It is an old medicinal plant that contains bitter principles and tannins. In folk medicine the flowers are used in kidney and bladder tea because of their diuretic effect; they are also used for gout and gall stones.

Pussy Toes is a low growing, ground-cover plant often found in rock gardens. Its striking, silvery foliage shows to particular advantage in sunny positions, where it forms thick carpets. Antennarias are perennial and will live for several years (they are completely frost hardy). They have dainty umbels of blossom similar to Straw Flowers. The white-flowered *Antennaria dioica* is a reliable species. The varieties "Glande", "Rubra", and "Nywood" flower in various shades of red.

Pussy Toes prefers a rather dry position on fine scree and in full sun. Mats that have grown too large should be cut back in spring and dead flowers removed. The plant goes well with Houseleek, Rock Rose, Pinks, and Cotula.

Aquilegia

10 - 70 cm

IV-VIII

Columbine

This plant, belonging to the Buttercup family (*Ranunculaceae*), is represented by several indigenous species in Central Europe. Its striking, nodding flowers have earned it the common names of Columbine, Granny's Bonnets, and Doves-in-a-Ring.

The Latin name *Aquilegia* derives from *aquila*, the Latin word for "eagle," probably due to the fact that the crooked spur resembles the beak or talons of an eagle.

In the Early Middle Ages, the flowers and seeds of the plant were used as a remedy against abscesses, rashes, and cancer; in the Renaissance, *Aquilegia* was considered an aphrodisiac. The smaller species are particularly suitable for the rock garden.

They are especially effective in small, stony crevices or at the base of a rock. The relatively undemanding *Aquilegia* grows best in moist, light soil in partial shade. It often self seeds.

POPULAR SPECIES:

- AQUILEGIA ALPINA: this perennial, also known as Alpine Aquilegia, occurs on mountain slopes and alpine pastures in the high Alps and grows to a height of 8–28 in (20–70 cm). The dark-blue flowers appear from June through August.

- AQUILEGIA BERTOLONII: since this species is only about four inches (10 cm) tall, it is also known as the Dwarf Aquilegia. Its blue flowers appear from April into May. Its small size makes it especially suitable for rock gardens.

- AQUILEGIA EINSELEANA: this plant grows to about 8 in (20 cm) tall and is very dainty. Its dark-blue to blue-purple flowers can be enjoyed from June through July.

- AQUILEGIA DISCOLOR: the pale-blue and white flowers of this Spanish Dwarf Aquilegia bloom from May through June.

- AQUILEGIA FLABELLATA: at 4–6 in (10–15 cm) this perennial is relatively small and also classed as a dwarf species. The blue and white flowers appear from May through June. The variety "Nana Alba" has white flowers.

Arabis caucasica

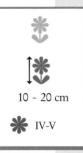

10 - 20 cm

IV-V

ROCKCRESS

Rockcress is distributed from the mountains of the eastern Mediterranean region to the Caucasus. One of the earliest plants to flower in our gardens, it is also one of the most beautiful, cushion-forming perennials in spring. As early as April and May it covers entire surfaces with cushions of white flowers.

Arabis is a classic rock garden plant. It only grows to a height of about eight inches (20 cm), but covers large areas or forms long cascades. It grows on walls, in cracks, in gravel, and between steps and terrace paving slabs—in short, anywhere where something needs to be covered or overgrown. It is also very good for edging paths.

Rockcress loves full sun, but will tolerate partial shade. In shade it will not flower so profusely, however, and growth will be less compact.

There are various species and varieties of Rockcress. The most well known, *Arabis caucasica*, has white or pink flowers. The variety "Schneehaube" has white flowers, while "Compinkie" has deep-pink flowers. Rockcress is often planted in conjunction with Moss Phlox, Aubrietia, Pinks, and Alyssum. The plants should be cut back after flowering.

Armeria

5 - 30 cm

✳ V-VII

Thrift

This plant belongs to the Leadwort family (*Plumbaginaceae*). It is particularly attractive on account of its hummocks of evergreen leaves. Depending on species, grass-like or needle-like leaves form dense, grassy cushions. When it flowers in the months of May through July, these cushions of foliage are completely covered in small, short-stemmed flowers in white or pink.

Thrift grows especially well on dry, salt-laden, sandy soils, on rocky ledges, and dry-stone walls. Its undemanding nature ensures its popularity and excellent suitability for the rock gar-

den, where it thrives in gravel beds or in cracks and crevices. It grows well with Houseleek, Saxifrage, Gentian, and Pinks. The plant needs a sunny position. Too much wet can be more damaging than drought, so it may need protection at particularly rainy times of year — by covering with a sheet of plastic, for example. It will survive for several years in soil that is not too rich. Old plants can be rejuvenated by division.

POPULAR SPECIES:

■ ARMERIA JUNIPERIFOLIA: this plant, also known as Dwarf Thrift, grows to a height of just two inches (5 cm). Depending on kind, the blooms range in color from white to various shades of pink. Examples of well-known varieties are the white-flowered "Alba" and deep-pink "Rubra" and "Suendermannii".

■ ARMERIA MARITIMA: this species occurs on salt marshes and cliffs on the coasts of Europe. It forms grassy cushions and grows to about six inches (15 cm). In this species, too, flower color varies according to kind: "Alba" has white flowers, "Dusseldorf Pride" deep-pink ones, and "Vesuvius" red ones.

Asphodeline lutea

80 - 100 cm

V-VI

Yellow Asphodel

The Asphodel belongs to the Lily family (Liliaceae) and grows naturally on sunny, dry, stony slopes in the Mediterranean area, making this species an obvious candidate for the rock garden.

The best-known species of Asphodel, and one that is particularly popular in the rock garden, is *Asphodeline lutea*. It is better suited to larger gardens, as it can attain the imposing height of 32–40 in (80–100 cm). It is therefore better to plant it at the edge, where it can spread out and develop its full potential. A sunny slope or any other position in full sun with a nutrient-rich soil is ideal.

The plant has narrow, three-sided, blue-green leaves that can be one foot (30 cm long). In the flowering period, from May through June, the Yellow Asphodel, also known as Jacob's Rod, produces spears of upright, yellow, star-shaped flowers, arranged in clusters. The plant is also very attractive in fall, with spikes of round seeds.

Asplenium trichomanes

15 - 30 cm

MAIDENHAIR SPLEENWORT

Asplenium trichomanes, also known as Maidenhair Spleenwort, belongs to the Spleenwort family (Aspleniaceae) and occurs as a number of different species all over the world. The pleasing appearance of ferns brings a tropical atmosphere to the rock garden. They can be planted on level ground or squeezed between rocks and into wall cracks. The smaller species, such as *Asplenium trichomanes*, are particularly suitable for this.

This fern occurs in temperate and sub-arctic zones on damp, shady cliffs, slopes, and tree stumps. Its long-lasting, matt-green fronds are pinnate, with rounded pinnae and glossy

black-brown midribs. It grows to a height of about 6–12 in (15–30 cm).

Like most ferns, the Spleenwort prefers a partially shaded to shady spot. It is not particularly demanding with regard to soil conditions, but does particularly well in a calcareous, loamy, humus-rich soil.

Well-known varieties include "Ramo Cristatum" and "Incisum".

Aster dumosus

15 - 50 cm

IX-X

BUSHY ASTER

The asters are a genus of many species occurring worldwide and belonging to the Composite or Aster family (Asteraceae). The Latin name Aster is derived from the word astrum, meaning "star" or "constellation". This refers to the radial arrangement of the ray and disk flowers of this genus. With their multiplicity of species, the fall flowering asters are especially interesting: blooming between September and October, they

beautify the rock garden at this late time of year.

Depending on species and variety, this perennial grows 10–20 in (25–50 cm) tall. The flowers form spherical cushions. The plant is very easy to care for and thrives in almost any position, but especially in the sun.

POPULAR VARIETIES:

■ HERBSTPURZEL: small, bluish-violet flowers; just 6 in (15 cm) in height.

■ LADY IN BLUE: blue flowers; up to 12 in (30 cm) in height.

■ ROSENWICHTEL: deep-pink flowers; up to 8 in (20 cm) in height.

■ HERBSTGRUSS VOM BRESSERHOF: pink flowers; at 16 in (40 cm) is slightly taller than the previous varieties.

■ JENNY: violet-purple flowers; up to 16 in (40 cm) in height.

■ KRISTINE: white flowers; up to 12 in (30 cm) in height.

Astrantia

30 - 80 cm

V-IX

MASTERWORT

Masterwort belongs to the Carrot family (Apiaceae). In Europe, its area of distribution stretches from Spain through the Balkans to the Caucasus. In the Alps it is often found at altitudes of up to 6,500 ft (2,000 m).

The particular beauty of this wild perennial is due to the unusual, star-shaped construction of its flowers: the many small, individual flowers are actually quite insignificant, but they are surrounded by a ring of pointed, pink and white bracts, just like an elegant ruff, giving the flower the appearance of a star.

Occasionally gardeners look for plants that will live long and prosper in slightly more shady positions. Masterwort is one such plant. With sufficiently moist soil, it will also grow in a fairly sunny position.

A distinction should be made between Large and Small Masterwort. *Astrantia major* grows to a height of 20–32 in (50–80 cm); *Astrantia minor*, more suitable for smaller gardens, only grows to about 12 in (30 cm). There are various kinds in numerous shades of pink, white, and dark red. "Rosea", for example, is a hybrid growing to about 28 in (70 cm) with red-

A LITTLE GARDEN POETRY…

In his didactic poem entitled "The Alps", the Swiss botanist Albrecht von Haller (1708–1777) describes Masterwort in sensitive verse: "There a shining leaf, notched into fingers, casts its green reflection on a bright stream. A striped star encloses in rays of white the delicate snow of the flowers, infused with matte purple".

dish flowers, which is also suitable for damper positions, while "Primadonna" is another red-flowered variety.

Athyrium filix-femina

40 - 70 cm

LADY FERN

The various species of *Athyrium* occur worldwide in damp forests of the temperate and tropical regions. A particularly decorative species, well suited to the rock garden, is *Athyrium filix-femina*, also known as Lady Fern.

The mainly lanceolate, bi- to tripinnate, light green fronds of *Athyrium filix-femina* lend the plant special decorative value. It can have impressive growth, reaching heights of 16–28 in (40–70 cm). Lady Fern grows especially well in partially shaded to shady positions.

It thrives in moist soil, with poor tolerance of dry conditions. In the rock garden it is very well suited for planting in front of, beneath, or between other plants, and for pools and streams. Ferns are downright unbeatable when it comes to greening and enlivening shadier areas where little else will grow. Popular varieties of Lady Fern are "Frizelliae", 8–12 in (20–30 cm) in height with round pinnae and also known as Tatting Fern; "Minutissimum", a miniature type of the species that also only grows to 12 in (30 cm); and "Rotstiel", with striking red stalks and midribs.

Aubrieta

Purple Rockcress

Aubrieta belongs to the Mustard family (Brassicaceae, Cruciferae) and comes originally from the mountainous regions of Southern and Eastern Europe and the Middle East. The plant takes its name from Claude Aubriet, the French artist who painted it in the 17th century while on an expedition with a botanist.

Purple Rockcress forms dense, green cushions of small, spatulate, gray-haired leaves about 2–6 in (5–15 cm) high. A particularly attractive characteristic of *Aubrieta* is its superabundance of flowers. During its blooming season between April and June, the plants are completely covered in a mass of flowers: mostly blue and purple, but in several varieties also red and pink.

5 - 15 cm

IV-VI

In the rock garden this plant, flowering relatively early in the year, provides exquisite spring flowers. It is especially popular for the tops of walls and dry-stone walls. It goes well with different colored, cushion forming plants such as Iberis, Moss Phlox, and Alyssum. *Aubrieta* thrives best in a warm spot in full sun and in well-drained, nutrient-rich soil containing lime.

Besides the various species of *Aubrieta*, a large selection of hybrids is also available on the market.

POPULAR SPECIES:

- ▬ AUBRIETA GRACILIS: this delicate species grows to about two inches (5 cm) and bears violet-purple flowers.

- ▬ AUBRIETA DELTOIDEA: this species is the natural form for many hybrids. It has pink to violet-blue flowers and grows to about four inches (10 cm).

- ▬ AUBRIETA HYBRIDS: the varieties "Blue Emperor", "Doctor Mules", and "Schloss Eckberg" have bluish-violet through dark-violet flowers and grow to about four inches (10 cm). "Silberrand" has lavender-blue flowers and its leaves have a light-colored edge. "Red Carpet", "Rosengarten", "Rubinkissen", and "Feuervogel" have pink or maroon flowers.

Bellis

Daisy

The Daisy belongs to the Composite or Aster family (Asteraceae) and is indigenous to the whole of Europe. The common name Daisy stems from "day's eye", as the flower opens in the morning and closes in the evening and on cloudy days. The botanic name is derived from Latin: *bellis* means "beautiful" and *perennis* means "continuing through the years", or "perennial".

The wild form of the Daisy is often considered a weed in the garden, particularly on the lawn. It is also of less interest for the rock garden than the newer cultivated varieties. These include varieties with larger flowers, which can be double, white, pink, or red and, depending on the kind, can be enjoyed between March and September. The plants grow to a height of about 2–8 in (5–20 cm).

The best places for *Bellis perennis* in the rock garden are in groups in small, level areas or between paving stones. They are also suitable for planting in stone troughs. The Daisy prefers a sunny to partially shaded position and moist, nutrient-rich soil. Examples of well-known varieties are "Robella", "Habanera", "Pomponette", "Rob Roy", and "Dresden China".

5 - 20 cm

III-IX

Berberis

Barberry

Berberis or Barberry is a spiny shrub growing to a height of about 80 in (200 cm). This winter-hardy plant is cultivated for its bell-shaped flowers and its fruits. The yellow flowers hang in 2–3 in (5–7 cm) clusters. The ripe fruits are fleshy, blood red in color, and very sour. There are, however, numerous cultivated varieties with different characteristics (e.g., white fruits or dark-red leaves). Barberry contains poisonous alkaloids, particularly in its leaves and bark.

As a deciduous or evergreen shrub, Barberry, along with conifers, adds interest to the garden in winter. The most suitable species and varieties for the rock garden are those that do not exceed 80 in (200 cm) in height. Some of these are dwarf shrubs that grow no higher than 12 in (30 cm).

■ BERBERIS BUXIFOLIA "NANA" (top): the Box-leaved Barberry forms a small, rounded shrub that barely exceeds 20 in (50 cm) in height. Its yellow to orange flowers usually only appear after several years' growth. This variety is very easy to grow and versatile, and ideally suited for planting near paths.

■ BERBERIS THUNBERGII (bottom): there are several varieties of *Berberis thunbergii*. "Atropurpurea Nana" grows to a height of 24 in (60 cm); it has purple-red foliage that turns carmine red in fall. The flowers are yellow and the fruits coral red—a beautiful contrast against groups of white stones. The variety "Green Carpet" reaches a height of 40 in (100 cm); its green leaves turn orangey red in fall, the many flowers are yellow to reddish, and the longish fruits are light red. Finally, "Kobold" grows to 16 in (40 cm) and has dark-green leaves. It is characterized by particularly compact growth.

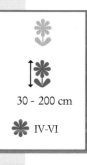

30 - 200 cm

IV-VI

Bergenia purpurascens

ELEPHANT EARS

With its large, paddle-shaped, leathery leaves, the evergreen *Bergenia* makes a useful contribution to any garden the whole year round. In addition, it is relatively easy to look after and fairly undemanding with regard to soil. This makes it a very popular rock garden plant.

This attractive perennial has a robust, creeping rootstock. In spring, between March and May, fleshy stalks appear, holding panicles of many individual, bell-shaped flowers above the leaves. Depending on species and variety, the flowers are red, pink, or white.

Bergenia prefers a sunny to partially shaded position. The plants grow particularly well in moist, humus-rich, well-drained soil, but will also succeed in more inhospitable conditions. These robust plants are useful as ground cover.

One example of a Bergenia species is *Bergenia purpurascens*. The attractive, dark-green leaves of this species are purplish red on the underside; in winter, the whole leaf turns red. The flowers, also purplish red, appear from April through May. The plant grows to a height of about 18 in (45 cm).

30 - 50 cm

IV-V

Blechnum spicant

20 - 70 cm

DEER FERN

Blechnum spicant belongs to the family of Water Ferns or Hard Ferns (*Blechnaceae*) and occurs in Europe, Asia, North Africa, and North America. In the wild it is found in raw humus soils, by streams, and in damp places.

Ferns are very attractive plants, ideal for the shadier parts of the rock garden. They grow well, for example, in the shade of rocks or shrubs. A pleasing effect can be produced by planting several examples of one species in small groups.

The evergreen Deer Fern is distinguished by elegant, upright growth and graceful fronds. The sterile fronds are about 8–16 in (20–40 cm) long and up to 2 in (4 cm) wide and simply pinnate. They are dark green and shiny and have a leathery appearance. Young plants form regular rosettes that spread out flat. Older plants develop fertile fronds that can grow to 28 in (70 cm) in length.

Blechnum spicant grows best in a partially shaded to shady position. It prefers moist, acid, lime-free soil and loves high air humidity.

Briza media

20 - 60 cm

V-VIII

QUAKING GRASS

Quaking Grass is one of the most attractive plants in the Grass family (*Poaceae*). A naturally occurring meadow grass, it is native to Europe in the form of several different species, although this formerly common, ornamental kind has become very rare. The grass, which grows in loose tufts, forms flowering stalks up to 24 in (60 cm) tall in May and June. The beautiful, heart-shaped, purple-brown spikelets are borne until August. One stalk can have as many as fifty individual spikelets. Quaking Grass is so named because the flower head seems to quake or tremble at the slightest breath of air.

Quaking Grass prefers a sunny position and well-drained soil. In the rock garden this filigree grass produces an ever-changing picture. It grows well with Moss Phlox, Lemon Thyme, various heathers, and other grasses. One Mediterranean species is *Briza maxima*, or Pearl Grass. It has particularly large spikelets and is also ideally suited for bouquets. For drying, Quaking Grass should be cut before it is ripe, then dried upright.

Buddleia

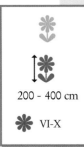

200 - 400 cm

VI-X

Butterfly Bush

Buddleia is also known as the Butterfly Bush, a name it richly deserves as the nectar-rich flowers attract a profusion of butterflies during the summer. The genus includes about 100 different species, in part evergreen shrubs or small trees distributed across Asia, Africa, and North and South America.

The plant is particularly popular for its long clusters of tiny, tubular, mainly fragrant flowers. Depending on species and variety, they appear between June and October, their color palette ranging from pink and violet through orange to yellow.

The plant loves a position in full sun and a rich, well-drained soil. The Butterfly Bush is an attractive addition to any rock garden. Since it can grow very tall, however, it is better suited to large gardens.

One well-known and popular species is *Buddleia alternifolia* (left). This deciduous shrub has slim, arching branches and dark-green to silvery-green, lanceolate leaves. It grows to a height of about 160 in (400 cm) and bears pale-violet flowers in June. The most common species is *Buddleia davidii* (bottom).

Calamintha

20 - 50 cm

V-IX

CALAMINT

Calamintha, also known as Calamint, belongs to the Mint family (*Labiaceae*). It occurs in dry, deciduous forests, on limestone rocks, and scree in the mountains of southwestern Europe and Asia Minor.

The botanical name *Calamintha*, which means "beautiful mint", does the plant justice: even though its rather small flowers are not conspicuously beautiful, the whole plant presents a very pleasing aspect with its barely branching, upright growth and the harmonious combination of leaves and flowers.

One species especially suited to the rock garden is *Calamintha grandiflora*, also known as Large-Flowered Calamint. It grows to a height of about 20 in (50 cm) and, depending on variety, produces pink to purple flowers between May and September.

Its leaves exude the aromatic scent of mint. The flowers form loose clusters in the leaf axils and combine with the leaves to form a loose bush. This easy-care plant prefers well-drained soil and should be given a warm, sunny to partially shaded position.

Calamintha grandiflora can be grown on any largish surface in the rock garden. It is equally attractive in gravel and scree beds and on dry-stone walls and terrace ledges.

One well-known and popular variety of this species is "Variegata" (bottom). It bears pink flowers and has finely variegated white and green foliage, forming an attractive contrast. The plant grows to a height of 8–16 in (20–40 cm).

Campanula

BELLFLOWER

Campanula, also known as Bellflower, belongs to the Large Bellflower family (*Campanulaceae*) and comes originally from rocky crevices and scree slopes in the mountains of Europe, including the Carpathians and the Caucasus. Both the common name and the botanical name, *Campanula*, which comes from the Latin and also means "bell", refer to the beautiful shape of the flowers.

The plants have heart-shaped to lanceolate leaves, which in some species are covered in dense hairs. The flowers are bell-shaped, sometimes also star-shaped, and can be blue, purple, white, or pink.

Depending on species and variety, they flower between May and September.

Many perennial *Campanula* species occur in the wild on Alpine scree or rocky slopes. This makes them eminently suitable for the rock garden, where they have many uses: they make themselves at home in rocky crevices, joints between slabs, cracks in walls, on the tops of walls, or in scree. They prefer a sunny to partially shaded position and thrive in well-drained, moderately dry soil. In other respects, Bellflowers are rather undemanding, easy plants, although you should keep a lookout for snails, which have a particular liking for them.

POPULAR SPECIES:

10 - 100 cm

V-IX

- CAMPANULA CARPATICA: this species is also known as Carpathian Bellflower. It grows to a height of six inches (15 cm) and has large, open, bell-shaped flowers.

  Popular blue-flowered varieties are "Blue Clips", "Blaumeise" ("Blue Titmouse"), and "Karpatenkrone"; well-known white-flowered varieties are "White Clips", "Silberschale", and "White Star".

- CAMPANULA GLOMERATA: this species, also known as Clustered Bellflower, can grow to a height of 20 in (50 cm); the dwarf variety "Acaulis" only reaches six inches (15 cm) and has dark-blue flowers. "Schneehäschen" and "Schneekissen" have white flowers.

- CAMPANULA PERSICIFOLIA (right): this species is also known as Peach-Leaved Bellflower. It can grow to a height of 32 in (80 cm).

  The dwarf form, *Campanula persicifolia f. nitida*, only reaches a height of 6–8 in (15–20 cm) and is available with white or blue flowers.

- CAMPANULA PORTENSCHLAGIANA: this species comes from Dalmatia and is also known as Dalmatian Bellflower. *Campanula portenschlagiana* grows to about 4–6 in (10–15 cm). One well-known variety is the dark-blue flowered "Birch Hybrid" (see photo p. 97, bottom).

Carex

SEDGE

Carex, also called Sedge, occurs naturally mainly in marshes, moors, and bogs, or beside water. The plant's main attraction lies in its patterned or colored leaves. In some species the flower spikes are also highly decorative.

This grass-like perennial has long, narrow leaves and individual yellow-brown flower spikes. Depending on species and variety, Sedge can grow to 4–60 in (10–150 cm).

One very beautiful species is *Carex muskingumensis* (right), also known as Palm Sedge. This deciduous perennial, which grows in loose tufts, has upright shoots with narrow, bright-green, lateral leaves radiating from them. In summer, from approximately July through August, it bears spikes of golden-brown to red-brown flowers. It can reach a height of 24–30 in (60–75 cm).

Carex muskingumensis prefers a sunny to partially shaded position and grows best in moist, fertile soil. In the rock garden it is suitable as ground cover or for underplanting taller shrubs that are bare at the base. A particularly beautiful effect can be achieved by planting Palm Sedge at the edge of a pond.

60 - 75 cm

VII-VIII

Caryopteris

60 - 100 cm

VII-IX

BLUEBEARD

Caryopteris is a small shrub belonging to the Verbena family (*Verbenaceae*) and is native to Mongolia and Northern China.

The blue to violet-blue flowers appear from July through September and form an interesting contrast to the longish, gray-green leaves. The plant has spreading, bushy growth and reaches a height of about 32–40 in (80–100 cm). A particular characteristic of Bluebeard is the spicy, lemony, aromatic fragrance of the leaves.

In the rock garden the pretty blue flowers of Bluebeard provide attractive late summer color. It does especially well in a sunny, sheltered position and prefers light, well-drained soil. The top growth can be killed by frost in a hard winter, but the plant will send out new shoots if cut back in early spring.

One of the most well known, and probably also one of the most attractive, cultivated varieties is "Heavenly Blue". It has particularly striking, violet-blue flowers and grows to about 24–40 in (60–100 cm). In the rock garden it is especially well suited for edging.

Centranthus ruber

30 - 70 cm

VI-IX

RED VALERIAN

Valerian belongs to the Valerian family (*Valerianaceae*). It is a native of the Mediterranean region of western and southern Europe, where it grows in dry places and on sunny roadsides. It brings a touch of Mediterranean flair and a holiday atmosphere to the garden.

Valerian is especially prized for its non-stop flowering. From June through July, the blue-green leaves of the plant, which grows to a height of about 24–28 in (60–70 cm), are complemented by panicles of deep-pink flowers in which the spur is twice as long as the ovary. They are particularly striking against light-colored rocks. It is essential to cut Valerian back after the first flowering as this ensures a second flush of flowers from August through September.

In the rock garden Valerian is ideally suited for dry-stone walls. It will even find a foothold and grow in chinks in mortared walls. It prefers a sunny position and a calcareous soil. It grows well with Cat Mint and Coreopsis and creates an impressive picture with green, cushion-forming plants.

Two varieties of Valerian are the scarlet "Coccineus" and the white-flowered "Albiflorus".

Cerastium tomentosum

10 - 15 cm

V-VI

SNOW-IN-SUMMER

Snow-in-Summer belongs to the Pink family (*Caryophyllaceae*) and is distributed throughout the world, being particularly plentiful in Europe and Asia. The name Snow-in-Summer refers to the mass of white flowers that appear in early summer.

The plant sends out runners and grows vigorously, making it excellent for ground cover. The dense, silvery-gray leaves give the impression of a silver carpet, which is completely covered with white flowers during the flowering period of May through June. The carpet of leaves grows no higher than 4–6 in (10–15 cm), but the plant does make a lot of horizontal growth. This should be kept in mind when planting, as it needs a lot of room.

Cerastium tomentosum is well suited for the rock garden, as this species has slightly better manners than some of the other species. It comes originally from Italy, grows to about 4–6 in (10–15 cm), and has white flowers.

It can be used to fill the gaps between paving stones and is also very attractive in walls. Suitable neighbors include Campanula, Speedwell, and Moss Phlox. Undemanding Snow-in-Summer prefers a position in full sun, with well-drained soil.

Chamaecyparis

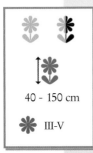

40 - 150 cm

III-V

CYPRESS

Next to the cedars, the cypresses are probably among the most noble conifers. In the Shinto religion of East Asia the Hinoki, a dwarf form of *Chamaecyparis*, is one of the five holy trees. Cross breeding has produced a wide range of forms of this genus, the low-growing, spreading species of which are particularly attractive for the rock garden.

All cypresses are characterized by small, soft, wedge-shaped, scaly leaves. These are arranged in flat, spreading, fan-shaped sprays and can have different coloration depending on species and variety. In *Chamaecyparis obtusa "Nana"*, the Dwarf Hinoki Cypress, the scaly needles are bluish green and the sprays rounded and undulating, like a shell. Other well-known species of Cypress include *Chamaecyparis pisifera* (Sawara Cypress) and *Chamaecyparis lawsoniana* (Lawson Cypress). The scaly needles of the latter are golden yellow to bluish green.

Cypresses flower between March and May, and the shape of the trees varies from spherical to conical. The smaller varieties, which are especially suitable for the rock garden, grow to 16–60 in (40–150 cm), while the larger varieties can shoot up to 65 ft (20 m).

The plant loves a sunny to partially shaded position on well-drained soil and should be protected from drying winds.

Chionodoxa

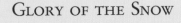

GLORY OF THE SNOW

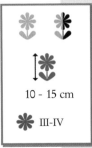

10 - 15 cm

III-IV

Glory of the Snow belongs to the Hyacinth family (*Hyacintha-ceae*) and comes from Asia Minor and Asia. It grows to a height of about six inches (15 cm), its flowers being star shaped and bright blue with a white eye in the center. It grows best in partial shade under trees and shrubs, but a sunny spot is also suitable. The soil should be well-drained, but moist, and rich in humus.

One of the best-known species of Glory of the Snow is *Chionodoxa sardensis* (right). It has gentian-blue flowers, with the flower stalks taking on a slight reddish tinge in sunny posi-tions. *Chionodoxa lucilia* has slightly smaller, sky-blue flowers. Both species look very pretty with snowdrops and crocuses, and the attractive blue flowers are also seen to good advantage in combination with bright-yellow daffodils. Glory of the Snow can self-seed very freely, so it is advisable to remove the seed capsules immediately after flowering. One variety that does not self-seed quite so vigorously is "Rosea". This variety has flowers up to two inches (4 cm) in size in soft, dusky pink.

Chrysanthemum

CHRYSANTHEMUM

10 - 70 cm

VI-IX

Chrysanthemum is a genus with many species in the Composite or Aster family (*Asteraceae*). The botanical name is derived from the Greek words *chrysos* and *anthemon* meaning "gold" and "flower" respectively, so it could be translated as "golden flower".

The plants either grow by creeping underground or forming small cushions. Depending on species and variety, the dark-green leaves are toothed or pinnate, and the plant can grow to a height of 4–28 in (10–70 cm), according to species.

The plant does especially well in full sun, but should be watered freely when in growth. In the rock garden it is particularly effective for providing color to brighten up dark scree. Suitable companion plants are Pussy Toes and Bellflowers.

One very pretty species is *Chrysanthemum parthenium*, also known as Feverfew or Bachelor's Buttons. The plant forms round, compact bushes and has simple pinnate leaves. Its chamomile-like scent can be quite pungent at times. Feverfew can grow to a height of 24 in (60 cm).

Clematis

CLEMATIS

60 - 800 cm

V-X

Clematis is a genus with very many species and forms distributed throughout the world. Many are rampant climbers, others are shrubby plants.

In the rock garden, various species of *Clematis* can be used in a range of ways. They can be used to grow up and through large trees, for example, or as ground cover, like *Clematis recta* (bottom). The plants are especially popular for their (mostly) very attractive flowers that, depending on species and variety, appear between May and October.

The plants prefer a sunny to partially shaded position and a well-drained, humus-rich soil. They grow especially well when planted in the shade with their roots in cool soil.

POPULAR SPECIES:

- CLEMATIS MONTANA: this species is also known as the Anemone Clematis. A deciduous climber, it bears masses of white to creamy-yellow flowers from May through June. It is a rampant grower and can reach heights in excess of 26 ft (8 m). Well-known and popular varieties are the white-flowered "Alexander", the pale-pink flowered "Elizabeth", and the pink-flowered "Pink perfection".

- CLEMATIS TANGUTICA: this species, also known as Golden Clematis, Golden Virgin's Bower, and Old Man's Beard, is a vigorous, late-flowering climber. Its plentiful, bell-shaped, yellow flowers appear from June through September and ripen to equally decorative, fluffy seed heads. It can reach a height of 16 ft (5 m). The yellow, strongly scented variety "Aureolin" and the pale-yellow "Anita" are found in many rock gardens.

Cortaderia selloana

Pampas Grass

50 - 250 cm

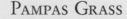 VIII-X

The exceptionally attractive Pampas Grass is native to South America and New Zealand. It is very long-lived and can become a real feature in the rock garden.

Cortaderia selloana forms dense tussocks of long, narrow, arching leaves that are light green and glaucous. The longish, silky, pinkish-white flowering plumes have high decorative value. Depending on variety, they appear between August and October. The plant can grow to the imposing height of 20–100 in (50–250 cm).

Pampas Grass prefers a warm, sunny spot in the rock garden. The soil should be well drained and rich in nutrients. The plant is sensitive to wet conditions in winter and should be given protection if necessary.

Popular varieties are "Pumila", which bears silvery-white flower plumes and grows to about 4 ft (1.2 m); "Sunningdale Silver," which has beautifully shaped, loose plumes in silvery white and grows to around 8 ft (2.5 m); and "Rosea", which bears very attractive pink plumes and reaches a height of 6 ½ ft (2 m).

Corydalis

Fumewort

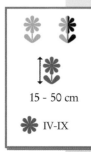

15 - 50 cm

IV-IX

Corydalis, also known as Fumewort, belongs to the Poppy family (*Papaveraceae*). In the wild this plant is found in light woods, underbrush, and on rocky slopes.

This attractive perennial is prized for its fine, green, pinnate foliage and the unusual shape of its flowers. The long, spurred, tubular flowers grow in racemes and are usually yellow, but can also be pink, lilac, white, or blue depending on species and vari-

ety. The flowering period is between April and September, with heights in the range of 6–20 in (15–50 cm).

In the rock garden *Corydalis* feels at home between narrow rocky crevices or on dry-stone walls. It can also be planted among shrubs. It tolerates sun, but prefers a position in partial shade. The soil should be well drained, but not too dry, and humus rich.

Popular species

- C. CASHMERIANA: this species has particularly attractive, clear blue flowers and reaches a height of about six inches (15 cm).

- C. CAVA: grows to a height of ten inches (25 cm) and has lilac-pink flowers. The variety "Alba" has white flowers.

- C. LUTEA: this species, also known as Yellow Corydalis, has golden-yellow flowers and grows to a height of about 8–16 in (20–40 cm).

- C. NOBILIS: this species is also known as Great-Flowered Fumewort. It has golden-yellow flowers and grows to about 12–20 in (30–50 cm).

- C. SOLIDA: this species, also known as Bird-in-a-Bush or Spring Fumewort, has pink, white, or purple flowers.

Cotinus coggygria

SMOKE TREE

200 - 500 cm

✳ VI-VII

The most striking feature of *Cotinus coggygria* is its long, feathery, fruiting plumes with their reddish hairs. They give the bush a light, airy appearance and produce the effect of a cloud of smoke, giving rise to its common name.

This bushy plant can reach the considerable height of 6½–16 ft (2–5 m). It has mid-green, oval leaves that turn an attractive yellow to orangey-red color in autumn. The tiny, rather inconspicuous, yellow-green flowers appear between June and July. The plant, however, only becomes a real eye-catcher when the airy, reddish, fruiting plumes develop from July onward.

The Smoke Tree grows best in a warm, sheltered, sunny position in calcareous, well-drained, but moist, soil. The plant is best used as a specimen tree and also looks good against natural stone walls. One very beautiful variety is "Royal Purple". Its dark purple-red foliage, turning scarlet in the fall, has earned it the name of Royal Purple Smoke Tree. It goes well with green and yellow-leaved shrubs, forming beautiful contrasts.

Cotoneaster

Cotoneaster

20 - 150 cm

❋ V-VI

Cotoneaster belongs to the Rose family (*Rosaceae*). There are many different species of this plant and they are often difficult to distinguish from one another. They mainly have small, white, or red flowers that subsequently develop into red berries. All parts of the plant, but especially the berries, are poisonous. Besides the well-known species *Cotoneaster microphyllus* and *Cotoneaster praecox*, other species such as *Cotoneaster dammeri* and *Cotoneaster horizontalis* are particularly well suited for the rock garden.

Popular species:

■ COTONEASTER DAMMERI (left): this species is also known as Bearberry Cotoneaster. It is well suited as ground cover or filler and grows to a height of about 8–40 in (20–100 cm). The plant grows particularly well in a sunny position, and has white flowers and attractive red fruits. Well-known varieties are "Coral Beauty", "Jürgl", and "Streibs Findling". The leaves assume beautiful fall tints.

COTONEASTER HORIZONTALIS: the branches of this species, also known as Rockspray Cotoneaster, grow horizontally in a herringbone arrangement, the pinkish-white flowers and beautiful, dark-red fruits being particularly striking and attractive. The plant grows to a height of about 40–60 in (100–150 cm) and should be planted in a sunny position. It acquires attractive red tints in the fall (bottom).

Cyclamen purpurascens

Cyclamen

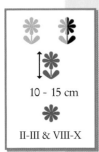

10 - 15 cm

II-III & VIII-X

Most people will be familiar with the Cyclamen as a pot plant, but there are also a few species that are winter hardy and grow well outside. *Cyclamen purpurascens*, formerly called *Cyclamen europaeum*, occurs mainly in the mountains of southern Europe, but it also grows in the Berchtesgaden Land area of southeastern Bavaria. Wild sites, however, are very rare and protected.

The sweetly scented flowers of the hardy Cyclamen consist of five, elegantly swept-back (reflexed), twisted petals. Its unmistakable flower shape inspired some of the Art Nouveau artists. The flowers are pink, more rarely white. It is not only the delightful flowers, however, that ensure the particular charm of this plant, which grows to a height of just 4–6 in (10–15 cm). The foliage is also very attractive—the rounded to kidney-shaped leaves are often marbled with silver on the upper surface, while the underside is usually purple-red.

These charming, tuberous plants grow well in partial shade and are therefore ideally suited for underplanting trees and shrubs, bringing color to the darker corners of the garden. Planted in humus-rich, well-drained, calcareous soil they will self-seed and, in time, can form a dense carpet of flowers. They go well with Spring Snowflakes, small shrubs, and ferns.

Besides *Cyclamen purpurascens*, two other species, which are also reliably winter hardy, are recommended for the rock garden:

- CYCLAMEN COUM: this species sometimes flowers as early as February. Flower color varies from white to dark carmine.

- CYCLAMEN HEDERIFOLIUM: the flowers of this species, in deep pink, pink, or white, appear from September until the first frost.

Cymbalaria muralis

Ivy-Leaved Toadflax

5 - 10 cm

VI-X

Cymbalaria muralis, Ivy-Leaved Toadflax, is also known by the botanical name *Linaria cymbalaria*. It comes originally from Northern Italy and the Northern Adriatic region. Since it grows naturally on dry-stone walls and in rocky areas, it can also be used for the rock garden.

In a sunny position the plant will form dense, compact carpets of short-stemmed leaves, which can reach a height of about 2–4 in (5–10 cm), covered in small lilac and yellow flowers resembling tiny snapdragons. The long flowering period, from June through October, makes the Ivy-Leaved Toadflax a particularly popular ornamental plant. It grows happily on shady or sunny walls, in rocky crevices, and on scree.

Ivy-Leaved Toadflax is very versatile in the rock garden: it can be used as flowering ground cover, for planting in wall crevices, or for growing between paving slabs. It is also suitable for troughs and tubs.

Well-known varieties are the white-flowered "Alba" and the compact, tuft-forming variety "Globosa".

Cytisus decumbens

Prostrate Broom

15 - 50 cm

V-VI

The Prostrate or Creeping Broom is a plant with wide distribution from Albania through Italy to France, where it grows on calcareous soils. It is winter hardy and drought resistant and grows best in a dry position in full sun.

Cytisus decumbens is a charming little shrub. The plant only grows to a height of 6–8 in (15–20 cm), but spreads out horizontally over time. In the rock garden, the Prostrate Broom can be used to good advantage as its long shoots can cover large, rocky surfaces. For this reason it is only recommended for larger gardens. The procumbent, spreading branches of the shrub have attractive gray-green leaves that form dense mats, while a profusion of golden-yellow flowers appears in summer.

Cytisus decumbens is particularly well suited for growing in dry-stone walls; it also grows well in limestone crevices, not spreading out quite so much in such positions. Another species of Creeping Broom recommended for the rock garden is *Cytisus kewensis*, or Kew Broom. This species produces creamy-white or pale-yellow flowers in spring. The plant does not exceed a height of 20 in (50 cm), but can cover an area of 44 ft½ (2 m½).

Daphne cneorum

Garland Flower

Daphne belongs to the Daphne family (*Thymelaeaceae*). The name, which comes from the Greek and means "laurel", refers to the great similarity of the leaves of some of the species of Daphne to laurel leaves. The seeds, bark, and other parts of the plant are very poisonous.

10 - 30 cm

IV-VI

Daphne grows wild on rocky slopes, making it ideal for the rock garden. The prostrate species of the genus make good ground cover. Daphne prefers a sunny to partially shaded position protected from wind and a well-drained but moist, humus-rich, calcareous soil.

One well-known and popular species is *Daphne cneorum*, also known as the Garland Flower, probably because the slender stems look like garlands when in flower. This evergreen shrub grows to a height of about 4–12 in (10–30 cm) and forms a low cushion. The strongly scented pink flowers appear from April through June and can bloom so profusely that the leaves of the plant are hardly visible. The Garland Flower is especially suitable for planting in rocky crevices and the gaps in dry-stone walls.

Dianthus

Pinks

10 - 30 cm

V-IX

These "divine flowers" of the Ancient Greeks, a sentiment still expressed in the botanical name today, have enchanted people from time immemorial. While the long-stemmed, cultivated garden species have established their position in floristry as cut flowers, the many species of Alpine Pinks are indispensable for the rock garden.

The choice of plants is large and can satisfy every demand. There are Pinks in the most varied colors and forms, suitable for every rock garden. You can choose between white, red, pink, double and single, dwarf and tall species. Particularly recommended are the undemanding dwarf species that grow well in any soil and form large cushions. All, however, require good drainage, humus-rich soil, and plenty of sunshine.

Popular species:

▬ DIANTHUS BARBATUS (right): this biennial species, also known as Sweet William, grows to 16 in (40 cm) and has different colors of flower depending on variety.

■ DIANTHUS ARENARIUS: this species, known as the Sand Pink, is widely distributed, particularly in Eastern Europe. It grows in sandy soils, often in pine forests, and loves sunny places. This cushion-forming plant sends out 4–12 in (10–30 cm) shoots, which mostly bear one or two flowers. These are white, often with a green eye and deeply fringed petals. One well-known, very deeply fringed variety is "Schneeflocke".

■ DIANTHUS DELTOIDES (top left): the Maiden Pink is widely distributed in Europe and Asia. This easy species is very well suited for the rock garden. It has green, grassy foliage and grows to a height of six inches (15 cm). The varieties "Brilliant", "Nelli", "Splendens", and "Leuchtfunk" have red flowers with a ring around the eye; "Alba" is a white-flowered variety.

■ DIANTHUS PLUMARIUS (bottom left): this very reliable plant is probably the most well-known species of Pink: the strongly scented Feathered or Cottage Pink. It has many different varieties in all gradations of color between red, pink, and white. The variety "Diamant" grows to a height of 12 in (30 cm), with double, white flowers; "Heidi" grows to eight inches (20 cm) and has double, blood-red flowers; "Ine" has semi-double, white flowers with a red ring and grows to 12 in (30 cm); "Pike's Pink" has double, pink flowers and grows to eight inches (20 cm).

DIANTHUS CHINENSIS: the bushy Chinese or Indian Pink grows to a height of about eight inches (20 cm). Two popular varieties are "Fire Carpet" with bright red flowers and the purple-flowered "Purpur".

Diascia barberae

15 - 30 cm

VI-IX

TWINSPUR

The botanical name of the genus *Diascia* is derived from the Greek: *di* meaning "two" and *askos* meaning "pouch" or "sac". This refers to the two spurs containing nectar at the back of the flower. There are about 50 species of *Diascia*, often very difficult to distinguish from each other. The plant is native to South Africa.

One popular species, which also often forms the basis for hybrids, is *Diascia barberae*. This plant grows to a height of about 6–12 in (15–30 cm). It is relatively undemanding and very free flowering, making it a popular rock garden plant. Its ½ inch (2 cm) pink flowers appear in terminal racemes between June and September. *Diascia* is such an attractive annual that it is worth sowing the seeds every year or overwintering rooted cuttings.

Diascia grows best in a sunny position. The soil should be moist, fertile, and well drained. Attractive varieties include the six inches (15 cm), salmon-pink "Ruby Field" and the ten-inch (25 cm) "Blackthorn Apricot" (right) with apricot-colored flowers.

Digitalis

Foxglove

Digitalis was known as a medicinal plant as early as the 18th century and was one of the first to be used for medicinal purposes in modern times. Although the plant is very poisonous, reduced doses of the Common or Purple Foxglove (*Digitalis purpurea*) are used in cardiac remedies.

Both the botanical name *Digitalis*, derived from the Latin word for "finger", and the common name Foxglove refer to the characteristic shape of the flowers. The plant is native to Europe, North Africa, and Western Asia.

The species grow best in a sunny to partially shaded position in well-drained soil that is moist and humus rich.

Its beautiful, strikingly shaped flowers make the Foxglove an attractive addition to any garden. The two following species are of special interest for the rock garden:

- DIGITALIS GRANDI-FLORA: this species is also known as the Yellow Foxglove. The plant grows to a height of about 35 in (90 cm) and is therefore better suited to the larger rock garden. The leaves are lanceolate and irregularly toothed. The wide, tubular flowers have turned-back edges with pointed tips and appear from June through September. They are pale yellow and netted with brown inside.

- DIGITALIS PURPUREA: this species is also known as the Common or Purple Foxglove. This biennial plant can grow to a height of 50 in (130 cm). The lanceolate, long-stalked leaves grow alternately on each side of the stem. The wild plants have purple flowers, but cultivated plants with white or pink flowers are also available. The flowering period is between June and July. One well-known variety is the white-flowered "Alba".

70 - 180 cm

VI-IX

Doronicum orientale

LEOPARD'S BANE

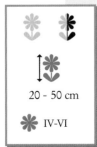

20 - 50 cm

IV-VI

Leopard's Bane, originally from southeastern Europe, is a particularly sunny spring flower. Golden-yellow flowers, reminiscent of marguerites or daisies, rise above the fresh, green foliage. Depending on variety, they appear singly, or more rarely in twos, on each stalk. The species of *Doronicum* differ essentially in the height of their flower stalks, which can vary between 8–20 in (20–50 cm). They are also good for cutting, bringing the feel of meadow flowers into your home.

In the rock garden, *Doronicum* is a relatively undemanding perennial, growing best in sun and partial shade. In keeping with its natural habitat, it is suitable for planting in edge positions in the garden. Here it will announce the spring in company with primulas and perennial cornflowers. Particularly attractive effects can also be achieved by combining *Doronicum* with red tulips and blue

hyacinths. Since the foliage of Leopard's Bane turns yellow after flowering, summer-blooming species should be planted in front of it.

POPULAR VARIETIES:

- GOLDKRANZ: this variety only grows to a height of about 12 in (30 cm) and so is also well suited for smaller rock gardens. The flowers are bright yellow.

- GOLDZWERG: with ten-inch (25 cm) flower stalks and a clump of leaves only growing to a height of six inches (15 cm), this compact variety is even smaller than the previous one. It has golden-yellow flowers from April through May.

- FRÜHLINGSPRACHT: this variety is suitable for larger rock gardens. The clump of leaves grows to eight inches (20 cm) and the flower stalks up to 20 in (50 cm). The flowers are also golden yellow.

- MAGNIFICUM: this variety also has flower stalks of up to 16 in (40 cm) with golden-yellow flowers.

Dryas octopetala

MOUNTAIN AVENS

10 - 15 cm

VI-VII

This very attractive dwarf shrub has gleaming, silvery-white flowers. It occurs mainly in mountains above the tree line.

In the rock garden, this plant is well suited for places in which greenery is required all year round. It is recommended as ground cover in areas of scree and rock. Since it spreads quickly and can form extensive carpets, it is more suitable for larger gardens. Smaller types are also available, however. Mats that have become too large should be cut back in spring.

Mountain Avens has broad, oblong to ovate leaves, light-green on the upper side and white and felty underneath. Altogether it reaches a height of about 4–6 in (10–15 cm). A profusion of white, saucer-shaped flowers appears between June and July. Later in the summer these develop into gray, silky, fluffy seed heads, which are also very attractive. *Dryas octopetala* grows best in the sun, but can also tolerate partial shade. It prefers well-drained soil that is rich in nutrients.

Dryopteris

Buckler Fern

70 - 80 cm

The Male Fern (*Dryopteris filix-mas*) is native to the temperate zones of Europe, Asia, and America. The rootstock and leaf stalks of the Male Fern are poisonous, especially in young plants. Extracts from this plant were previously used as a remedy for tapeworm.

As a garden plant the Male Fern is very undemanding; it even tolerates dryness and will grow in practically any garden soil. With its pale-green fronds, often growing to hip height, it also looks very attractive in dark positions under trees.

OTHER SPECIES

■ DRYOPTERIS AFFINIS: the long fronds of the Golden or Scaly Male Fern have attractive golden-brown scales, especially noticeable when they are unfurling. This species grows to a height of about 32 in (80 cm).

■ DRYOPTERIS ERYTHROSORA: the Japanese Shield Fern has beautiful, orangey-red new growth in spring. After this it turns a deep green and grows to a height of 12–32 in (30–80 cm).

■ DRYOPTERIS SIEBOLDII: Siebold's Wood Fern has an unusual shape for a fern—its gray-green fronds are simple pinnate.

Eremurus

Foxtail Lily

100 - 200 cm

✳ VI-VII

With their towering flower spikes, the plants of the genus Eremurus, also known as Foxtail Lilies, are a very imposing and attractive sight. The various species come originally from dry grassland and semi-desert in Western and Central Asia and reach heights of 40–80 in (100–200 cm).

Since lower-growing species are better suited to the rock garden, *Eremurus stenophyllus*, which attains a height of only 40 in (100 cm), is particularly appropriate. This bushy perennial has narrow, strap-like, gray-green leaves, which can sometimes be very hairy. Its most decorative feature, however, is its dark-yellow flowers, which can be enjoyed between June and July. The plant prefers a sunny position and nutrient-rich, well-drained soil. You can achieve some really beautiful effects in the rock garden with Foxtail Lilies. They are shown to best advantage in small groups against evergreen trees or among medium-sized, herbaceous perennials. They look especially attractive when the graceful flower stalks sway gently in the breeze. One very popular and attractive subspecies is *Ex isabellinus*. It flowers in gleaming shades of yellow, orange, near red, and white.

Erica carnea

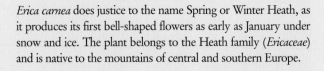

SPRING OR WINTER HEATH

15 - 30 cm

I-IV

Erica carnea does justice to the name Spring or Winter Heath, as it produces its first bell-shaped flowers as early as January under snow and ice. The plant belongs to the Heath family (*Ericaceae*) and is native to the mountains of central and southern Europe.

This pre-spring bloomer is of particular importance in the rock garden as it opens the flowering season along with many types of bulb. Winter Heath is very effective when planted among rocks and on the edge of the rock garden, where it can form a link with the neighboring beds. In addition, it makes an excellent ground cover plant.

This low-growing dwarf shrub reaches a height of about 12 in (30 cm). The many curving branches are densely covered with evergreen, needle-like, verticillate green leaves. The flowers are mostly flesh-colored, but there are other colors as well: examples include "Winter Beauty" (pink), "Rubra" (dark red), and "Springwood White" (white). Winter Heath grows best in a sunny place and prefers a chalky soil. It should be cut back after flowering so that it does not become leggy and bare at the base.

Eryngium

SEA HOLLY

GARDENING TIP

With its long flowering period, Sea Holly provides long-lasting decoration in the garden. It is also very good, however, for small dried-flower arrangements and bouquets. The best time for cutting is when the bracts surrounding the flowers have their strongest coloration, before the individual flowers have opened.

Eryngium is a genus of 230 annual, biennial, deciduous, and evergreen plants. They are widely distributed, but most of the cultivated species come from Eurasia and North and South America.

Sea Hollies are unusual, but strangely attractive plants. They form basal rosettes, often of the prickly leaves so typical of thistles, with silvery-white veins. The strong stalks, usually branched in the upper third, bear semi-spherical to cylindrical umbels of tiny, stalk-less flowers with prickly, silver-blue bracts of metallic sheen.

There is an abundance of Sea Holly species suitable for the rock garden. They are extravagant partners for filigree grasses and fine-leaved perennials, as they provide exciting contrasts. These mainly winter-hardy plants prefer a sunny position and light, well-drained soil. They should be well watered during growth, but otherwise kept dry.

POPULAR SPECIES

- ERYNGIUM PLANUM: the compact variety "Blue Dwarf" has many small, intensely violet-blue flowers and will enrich smaller flowerbeds for several years (it is completely frost hardy). It makes bushy growth up to 20 in (50 cm).

- ERYNGIUM BOURGATII: a clump-forming herbaceous plant with striking silvery veined, dark green leaves, which grows to a height of about 16 in (40 cm).

- ERYNGIUM AMETHYSTINUM: branching, silvery stalks with one-and-a-half (2–3 cm) long umbels. Its flowers are steely blue to violet and it grows to about 28 in (70 cm) in height.

- ERYNGIUM GIGANTEUM: this species, also known as Giant Sea Holly, has bracts with an ivory tinge. It forms cylindrical umbels of pale-green to blue flowers up to two-and-a-half (6 cm) long. It is frost hardy, growing to a height of up to 28 in (70 cm).

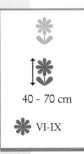

40 - 70 cm

VI-IX

Fargesia murielae

UMBRELLA BAMBOO

100 - 400 cm

The evergreen Bamboo species belonging to the genus *Fargesia* come originally from damp forests in central China and the northeast Himalayas.

One very well-known species is *Fargesia murielae*. This clump-forming Bamboo has yellow-green shoots, which turn yellow later and mostly branch in the first year. When in full leaf, they can bend over slightly under the weight of the small, bright green leaves. The culm sheaths are covered in downy hairs. The plant can reach a height of 40–160 in (100–400 cm).

Fargesia murielae prefers a sunny to partially shaded position. The soil should be moist and fertile: thus, this Bamboo can be planted near a pond. These evergreen plants bring a breath of the Far East into the rock garden and their gentle rustling in the breeze can conjure up a unique atmosphere.

Umbrella Bamboo is available in many different varieties. Well-known ones include "Jumbo", growing to 120 in (300 cm); "Dragon", also 120 in (300 cm); "Simba", at 60–100 in (150–250 cm); and "Bimbo", which only grows to 40–60 in (100–150 cm).

Festuca

FESCUE

10 - 40 cm

✿ VI-VII

The genus *Festuca*, also known as Fescue, includes about 300 to 400 different species, occurring in grassland, on the edges of woodland, and at the edge of water in temperate latitudes.

The plant is ideally suited for rock gardens, where it provides an attractive contrast to Alpine species. It feels at home in rocky crevices and gravel beds. Fescue prefers a position in full sun to partial shade and grows well in dry, well-drained soil.

POPULAR SPECIES

- **FESTUCA GLAUCA** (right): this species is also known as Blue Fescue for its characteristic blue-green leaves. This evergreen perennial grass forms a dense bushy tuft of slender, upright or arching, rolled leaves. The shortly branched panicles of blue-green flowers tinged with violet appear between June and July. This attractive grass grows to a height of about 8–16 in (20–40 cm). Examples of well-known varieties include "Azurit", which forms dense, deep blue cushions; "Harz", which has dark blue-green leaves; and "Blaufuchs", which forms steely-blue cushions.

- **FESTUCA SCOPARIA** (left): this species is also known as Bearskin Fescue and comes originally from the Pyrenees. This dense, cushion-forming evergreen grass has narrow, rolled, bright-green leaves and reaches a height of about 6–10 in (15–25 cm). It flowers between June and July.

Genista

BROOM

With its bright-yellow flowers, Broom is a popular messenger of spring. It is an easily grown and robust shrub with a profusion of blooms, which can occasionally be white or pink. There are many species of Broom, which can grow to a height of up to 80 in (200 cm), but dwarf forms more suitable for the rock garden are also available.

Genista lydia, a hardy dwarf broom, also known as Woadwaxen, is a cushion-forming deciduous shrub with arching, thorn-tipped branches. From May through June it bears short racemes of yellow, pea-shaped flowers about a half-inch (1.5 cm) long. It prefers warm, sunny positions with light, well-drained soil, moderately rich in nutrients. It is ideally suited for planting on dry-stone walls and embankments. *Genista lydia* grows to a height of approximately 20 in (50 cm).

Genista sagittalis, or Winged Broom, is a shrub that only reaches a height of 8–12 in (20–30 cm) and is therefore perfect for smaller rock gardens. The plant is prostrate with creeping branches that root as they spread. The upright stems have two broad, interrupted wings, and the golden-yellow flowers appear in June. A sunny position is essential. Winged Broom is ideal for planting on wall tops and is very well suited as a colonizing plant.

20 - 50 cm

V-VII

Broom feels particularly comfortable in a loamy, sandy garden soil, but does not tolerate wet roots. It is frequently used as the main plant in its group. Good companion plants include Erica, grasses, pines, junipers, and wild roses. It should be watered and fed sparingly and, after flowering, the plant should be cut back by a third. Other species recommended for the rock garden are *Genista hispanica*, *Genista pilosa*, *Genista umbellate*, and *Genista radiata*.

Gentiana acaulis

Gentian

"A good and glorious genus"—these were the words of Johann Wolfgang von Goethe on the subject of the Gentian. With its proverbial blue flowers the plant is a symbol of the Alps; hardly another plant has achieved such fame. The once common Gentian has become a very rare plant, however, and is now strictly protected. Incidentally, the famous Gentian schnapps is made from Yellow Gentian (*Gentiana lutea*).

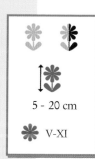

5 – 20 cm

V-XI

In the rock garden, too, the Gentian is a true classic. As a typical mountain plant it is mainly of significance for "natural" gardens. The low-growing, cushion-forming species spread among stones and rocks, forming pretty carpets. When deciding on the right species for a particular spot, it is necessary to distinguish between the chalk-loving, chalk-tolerant, and chalk-hating species. In the right place the plants are undemanding, but soil moisture should vary as little as possible.

The exquisite, bell-shaped flowers, which range from pale blue to ultramarine in the blue spectrum, delight from May through late fall. Combining them with grasses, Erica, and dwarf rhododendrons serves to emphasize the colors and shapes of the gentians themselves. Planting en masse shows the beautiful blue shades of the flowers to even better advantage.

POPULAR SPECIES

■ GENTIANA ACAULIS: the Trumpet or Stemless Gentian is one of the chalk-hating species. It forms splendid clumps with brilliant, deep-blue, starry flowers, spotted olive green inside. There is also a white flowered vari-

ety, "Alba". *Gentiana acaulis* flowers in May and June. It should be given a sunny position.

■ GENTIANA ANGUSTIFOLIA: as the Latin name indicates, this species has long, narrow leaves. It also has short flower stalks. It is chalk-tolerant and will also grow in either sun or partial shade. It flowers from April through May and mostly grows to a height of 3–4 in (7–10 cm). The bell-shaped flowers are dark blue. *Gentiana angustifolia* is an easy species to grow.

■ GENTIANA SINO-ORNATA: this chalk-hating species has its flowering period from September through November and is known as Fall Gentian. The flowers are a deep azure blue inside, duller on the outside, and with broad green-yellow stripes. *Gentiana sino-ornata* grows to a height of 8 in (20 cm). This very attractive plant is easy to grow on chalk-free soil.

Geranium

Crane's Bill

The distinctive shape of the seed heads that form once the *Geranium* has flowered give this plant the name Crane's Bill, being reminiscent of the head and bill of a crane. The various species of this genus, belonging to the Geranium family (*Geraniaceae*), are very versatile and can be used in the most varied garden situations. The smaller species, however, are of great interest for the rock garden.

These bushy perennials have circular, lobed leaves in green, silvery gray, or reddish brown. The rounded flowers appear in small, loose clusters and, depending on species and variety, are lilac pink, pale pink, carmine pink, or carmine red.

The plant prefers a position in full sun and well-drained, fairly dry, nutrient-rich soil. It feels at home in scree and crevices, and also in walls in sun to partial shade. Geraniums can be used to beautify dry-stone walls and terrace beds. Suitable neighbors include Campanula, Gentian, Saxifrage, and grasses.

Popular species:

■ GERANIUM ARGENTEUM: this species is also known as Silver-Leaved Crane's Bill on account of its silver-gray foliage. It has pale-pink flowers with a dark edge, and grows to a height of 4–6 in (10–15 cm).

■ GERANIUM DALMATICUM: this species is also called Dalmatian Crane's Bill. It has large, pink flowers and particularly attractive, red foliage in autumn. The plant grows to a height of about four inches (10 cm). The variety "Album" has white flowers.

■ GERANIUM RENARDII: this species, also called Renard's Crane's Bill, reaches a height of 12 in (30 cm) and has white, dark-veined flowers. The hairy, scalloped leaves are grayish green.

■ GERANIUM SANGUINEUM: this species is also known as Bloody Crane's Bill, an obvious reference to its crimson flowers. In addition, individual leaves turn blood red before they fall, providing interesting colour accents outside the flowering period. The plant grows to a height of about 8–20 in (20–50 cm).

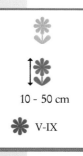

10 - 50 cm

V-IX

Gypsophila repens

CREEPING BABY'S BREATH

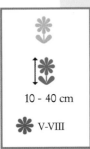

10 - 40 cm

V-VIII

Gypsophila repens is also known as Creeping Baby's Breath, a name that describes the plant's growth, forming as it does a creeping mat covered in a delicate mist of small, star-shaped flowers. This attractive and versatile plant grows naturally on scree fields and calcareous rocks in the mountains of central and southern Europe.

The mats or cushions of Creeping Baby's Breath can, depending on species and variety, grow to a height of 4–16 in (10–40 cm). Its lanceolate to needle-like leaves are green to grayish green and are also attractive outside the flowering period. The delicate, pinkish-white flowers appear between May and August.

This dainty beauty brings lightness and elegance to the rock garden. It is ideally suited for planting in walls, where it forms a delicate waterfall of flowers. The mist of flowers also presents a beautiful picture, spilling out of cracks and crevices or creeping over rocks.

Baby's Breath prefers a sunny position and thrives in well-drained, calcareous soil. It goes well with Pinks, Rock Roses, Saxifrage, St. John's Wort, and Campanulas.

One very popular, and very beautiful, variety is "Rosea". It has particularly dense growth and impressive, delicate pink flowers. It grows to a height of about four inches (10 cm). Other well-known varieties are "Rosa Schönheit", which has deep-pink flowers and compact growth, reaching a height of about six inches (15 cm), and "Rosenschleier", which has delicate pink flowers and reaches a height of 8–16 in (20–40 cm).

Helianthemum

ROCK ROSE OR SUNROSE

The Rock Rose is an evergreen or partly evergreen sub-shrub belonging to the Rock Rose family (*Cistaceae*), which occurs as numerous different species in Europe, Asia, and the Mediterranean region. Depending on variety, it grows to about seven inches (15–30 cm) and is ideally suited to rock gardens.

Its name clearly reflects what is especially important for this plant. Its botanical name is derived from the Greek words for sun (*helios*) and flower (*anthemos*), and the common name of Sunrose also expresses its preference for dry, sunny places.

The leaves of the Rock Rose are longish, strongly keeled, shiny green to silver gray, and hairy. The bushes bear round, saucer-shaped flowers, the colors of which vary, depending on variety, from white to yellow to red, with many nuances of shade in between. These easy perennials conjure up an exquisite blaze of color in the summer rock garden. Cutting back immediately after the main flush of flowers will ensure the plant produces many more blooms.

15 - 30 cm

V-VIII

It goes particularly well with Pinks, Outdoor Cacti, Houseleek, and Rue. Popular species are: *Helianthemum apenninum*, *Helianthemum nummularium*, *Helianthemum canum* (left), *Helianthemum lunulatum*, and *Helanthemum oelandicum*.

The following are well-known varieties of *Helianthemum* hybrids: the apricot-colored "Amy Baring", the red "Cerise Queen", the pale-yellow "Gelbe Perle", the pink varieties "Pink Double" and "Rosa Königin", the yellow "Sterntaler", and the white "Wisely White".

Hypericum

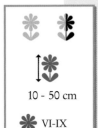

10 - 50 cm

VI-IX

St. John's Wort

St. John's Wort is in full bloom around the time of the summer solstice—near to St. John's day.

It is not only one of the most beautiful sun plants, but has long been prized for its medicinal properties. It was even believed to have magical powers, being said to drive away darkness and evil, keep demons at bay, and protect from thunderstorms.

The true St. John's Wort (*Hypericum perforatum*) is still used today as a remedy against mood swings, nerves, and mild depression.

The St. John's Wort genus includes various different species and varieties. *Hypericum calycinum* (Rose of Sharon) is particularly well suited for the rock garden. This evergreen sub-shrub, which spreads by sending out vigorous stolons, can reach a height of up to 20 in (50 cm). Its dense shoots and rapid growth make it well suited as a ground cover plant. The attractive, 2–3 in (5–7 cm), golden-yellow, cup-shaped flowers are borne from July through September.

St. John's Wort grows best in a sunny to partially shaded place in light, humus-rich soil. It goes well with robust plants such as Sea Holly and Blue Oat Grass. This frost-sensitive plant can die down in cold winters, but if the dead shoots are cut back hard in spring the shrub will regrow.

Other well-known species of St. John's Wort that are also suitable for the rock garden are *Hypericum olympiacum*, more suited for larger rock gardens with its round, thin shoots and lemon-yellow flowers, and the yellow *Hypericum polyphyllum*.

Iberis saxatilis

PERENNIAL CANDYTUFT

Low, evergreen clumps of *Iberis* or Perennial Candytuft can be found growing naturally in rocky places in southern Europe. This makes it a suitable plant for the rock garden.

The plant is characterized by robust growth and forms compact cushions, which attain a height of 4–10 in (10–25 cm). Its shoots are well branched and covered with lanceolate, smooth-edged, dark-green leaves. Numerous, small, spheroidal flower heads appear during the flowering period from April through May. The flowers are mostly white, but also pink in some species. The profusion of flowers and the evergreen leaves make species of Perennial Candytuft very popular in the rock garden. They are easy to grow, preferring full sun and well-drained, nutrient-rich soil, and virtually irreplaceable for rocky crevices, dry-stone walls, and troughs. Suitable neighbors include Aubrietia, Moss Phlox, and Saxifrage.

One especially popular species is *Iberis saxatilis*, also called Perennial Candytuft. The plant forms a cushion four inches (10 cm) high and has matte, dark green leaves. This attractive spring bloomer bears white flowers from April through May.

10 - 25 cm

IV-V

Iris germanica

Purple or London Flag

Iris is a genus of very many species and varieties within the Iris family (Iridaceae).

Botanically, the plant was named after Iris, the Greek goddess of the rainbow, undoubtedly in reference to the rainbow variety of its iridescent flower colors. Another name for the Iris is Sword Lily, an obvious reference to the pointed, sword-like, gray-green, upright leaves, which have a unique beauty. It is during the flowering period of April through June, however, that the plant really comes into its own, with its (usually) large, colorful, and strikingly beautiful flowers.

In the interpretation of dreams, the Iris symbolizes hope and good news. It can also stand for Christian faith and authority, and a stylized Iris can be seen on the Bourbon coat of arms.

The *Iris* genus can be roughly divided into two main groups—bulbous irises and rhizomatous irises. The latter group includes species of Bearded Iris, which have colored hairs on the falls; Beardless Iris; and Evansia or Crested Iris, which have crests on the falls.

The many different species of Bearded Iris are especially popular in gardens. These can also be divided into three different groups according to height: the Iris Barbata Eliator hybrids (Tall Bearded Iris) can grow to a height of more than 28 in (70 cm); the Iris Barbata Media hybrids (Intermediate Bearded Iris) reach heights of 16– 28 in (40–70 cm); and the Iris Barbata Nana hybrids (Dwarf Bearded Iris) only grow to about 8–12 in (20–30 cm).

The small Iris Barbata Nana hybrids are especially suitable for the rock garden, where they should be given a visible position so that their striking flowers can be seen to best advantage. They are attractive in areas of dry scree or against dry-stone walls. The especially dwarf forms are also ideally suited for troughs. They present an extremely harmonious picture in close proximity to grasses or Rock Roses.

The plants revel in full sun. The soil should be calcareous, rather dry, rich in nutrients, and well drained.

There is a rich variety of Iris Barbata Nana hybrids with an extensive color palette, ranging from white to violet and also multicolored. Plant breeders are actively engaged in developing these popular plants and the constant appearance of new varieties on the market makes it difficult to give a comprehensive overview. We nevertheless present a few examples to give some idea of the unbelievable diversity of color in this species.

Popular varieties

15 - 30 cm

✳ IV-VI

- CHERRY GARDEN: grows to a height of about 10–12 in (25–30 cm) and has dark purple to wine-red flowers.

- FIRESTORM: has burgundy-red flowers and grows to a height of about six inches (15 cm).

- GOLDGELB: has golden-yellow flowers and grows to a height of eight inches (20 cm).

- LILLY WHITE: has white flowers and reaches a height of up to eight inches (20 cm).

- MELON HONEY: grows to a height of about ten inches (25 cm) and has apricot-colored flowers.

- ROTE LATERNE: grows to about 10–12 in (25–30 cm) and has red-brown flowers.

- SAPPHIRE JEWELS: grows to ten inches (25 cm) and has sapphire-blue flowers.

Juniperus

JUNIPER

Juniperus communis, or Common Juniper, grows as a bush or tree and reaches a height of around 33 ft (10 m). Its natural habitats are light pinewoods, heaths, and sunny, rocky slopes. Incidentally, gin is distilled from the berries of the Common Juniper.

The evergreen Juniper is a popular and undemanding conifer for the rock garden. Which of the many different varieties you decide on depends on the way you want to use Juniper in the garden.

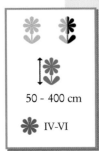

50 - 400 cm

IV-VI

POPULAR SPECIES

- HIBERNICA: the Irish Juniper with its slender, columnar growth reaches a height of up to 14 ft (4 m). It is most suitable as an accent plant.

- REPANDA: this low-growing variety of Common Juniper forms round cushions and has intensely green needles. With its dwarf growth, it colonizes even the closest fitting stone slabs.

SQUAMANTA: the Blue or Blue Star Juniper certainly does justice to its name—its small needles have an attractive, striking, silvery-blue coloration. Well-known varieties are "Blue Carpet", and "Blue Star", which with unimpeded growth can reach a height of 32–40 in (80–100 cm); they tolerate pruning well.

Lavandula

40 - 60 cm

VII-VIII

Lavender

The glorious fragrance of Lavender transports you to the South of France, where the plant grows in large fields and carpets of blue flowers envelop the whole district in their distinctive, aromatic perfume.

The name of this plant, which comes from the Mediterranean region, is derived from the Latin word *lavare* meaning "to wash", although this is attributed less to its cleaning properties than simply to its clear, fresh fragrance.

Lavender has long been known as a medicinal plant of old monastery and country gardens. From time immemorial, people have prized its antiseptic and calming effects, and it has been used as a remedy against sleeplessness, coughs, circulatory disorders, anxiety, and nervous disorders.

The fragrant flowers are not only used in the perfume industry: they can also be used as edible decorations with an aromatic, herbal taste.

Lavender has gray-green leaves that are white and felty underneath and roll in slightly at the edge. A lavender bush grows to a height of about 24 in (60 cm). Between July and August it bears blue-violet flowers in attractive spikes up to 16 in (40 cm) long.

Its long flowering period and undemanding growth make lavender an ideal plant for rock gardens, of which they have long been very popular occupants. The shrubs grow well in dry, chalky, stony soils and prefer a sunny spot protected from wind. Lavender is particularly effective in the rock garden when planted among stones or at edges and in combination with Fescue, Catmint, Verbascum, and Rock Roses.

One variety particularly suitable for rock gardens is "Hidcote Blue" (right), named for the famous English garden, Hidcote Manor. Its special characteristics are its compact, round, bushy, well-branched growth and sturdy, deep-violet to dark-blue flower spikes.

Liatris

BLAZING STAR OR GAYFEATHER

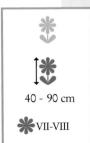

40 - 90 cm

VII-VIII

Liatris, also known as Blazing Star or Gayfeather, is native to eastern North America where it is found in prairies and woods in dry, stony soil.

This perennial plant forms clumps of simple, linear to lanceolate leaves, which can be covered in fine hairs. Between July and August tall spikes with numerous, downy flowers sprout up out of the clumps. Depending on species and variety, they provide a blaze of violet, purplish red, pinkish purple, or white. Unusually, the individual flowers on the spike open from top to bottom. Blazing Star can grow to a height of 16–36 in (40–90 cm). The plants grow well in a sunny position and prefer a moist, humus-rich, well-drained soil.

One of the best-known and most popular species is *Liatris spicata*. This perennial bears its long-lasting, pinkish-purple or white flower heads between July and August. It grows to a height of 16–36 in (40–90 cm) with a spread of up to 18 in (45 cm). Well-known varieties of this species include "Callepsis", with bright carmine-red flowers; "Kobold", with lilac to pinkish-purple flowers (16–20 in/40–50 cm); and "Floristan Weiss", with white flowers (24–36 in/60–90 cm).

Lithodora diffusa

LITHODORA

Lithodora diffusa, previously called *Lithospermum*, occurs naturally in pine forests, in shrubby areas, and on sandy soils. This pretty, evergreen shrub is cushion forming and reaches a height of about 6–8 in (15–20 cm). Its prostrate stems have small, flat, lanceolate leaves, which are longish to elliptical and dark green. Lithodora is particularly attractive during the flowering period from May through June, when it is completely covered in masses of funnel-shaped flowers in pure gentian blue.

Its spreading growth makes *Lithodora diffusa* par-

ticularly well suited to the rock garden as a ground-cover plant. Beautiful effects are also achieved when the stems can clamber over obstacles or rocks, and when they hang over the edges of trough gardens. The plant grows best in full sun, in nutrient-rich, totally lime-free soil.

One of the best-known and most popular varieties is the particularly free flowering "Heavenly Blue", with its very beautiful blue flowers. The variety "Grace Ward" has particularly large and intensely colored flowers. "Alba" has white flowers.

15 - 20 cm

V-VI

Lobularia maritima

Sweet Alyssum

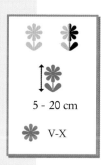

5 - 20 cm

V-X

Lobularia maritima is also known as Seaside Lobularia. Its other common name of Sweet Alyssum was undoubtedly acquired because of its pleasant scent, which resembles that of honey.

This annual plant forms flat cushions and reaches a height of about 2–8 in (5–20 cm). During the flowering period between May and October it produces a veritable sea of mostly white, but in some varieties also pink or violet, flowers.

This long-flowering summer bloomer can be used nicely in the rock garden to bridge areas with few other flowers or to fill gaps in the planting scheme at short notice. If, as in many rock gardens, the Alpine plants are the real attraction, summer flowers should be used quite sparingly so that they do not detract too much from the other plants. Sweet Alyssum is ideal as ground cover and is also suitable for planting in walls.

The plant prefers a sunny position, but will also succeed in partial shade. It tolerates stony subsoil and grows best on well-drained, rather poor, calcareous soil. The plant should be cut back after the first flush of flowers.

Lupinus

Lupin

40 - 120 cm

V-VII

Lupinus is a genus of over 200 species that are among the most colorful plants in the flower border. With their long, dense racemes of flowers they provide striking color effects and are splendid for combining with other plants. The distinctive colors can be used to create a fairy-tale atmosphere.

The Lupin family consists of perennials and annuals. They are all characterized by elegant, digitate leaves and slightly scented, butterfly-like flowers in cylindrical racemes.

Especially well-known and popular are the Russell hybrids, the most robust, winter-hardy Lupins for the ornamental garden. They form beautiful, dense clumps of light green leaves and flower from May through July.

Lupins vary in height from 32–48 in (80–120 cm) and the racemes of flowers can be up to 24 in (60 cm) long. Dwarf Lupins (Lupinus or Russell hybrids) are especially suitable for slightly smaller rock gardens. They grow to a height of about 16 in (40 cm), are just as vigorous as the larger species, and flower at least as profusely.

Lupins grow well in light, slightly acid soil with good drainage. A peculiarity of these plants is their ability to collect nitrogen from the air in their roots. In this way they enrich the soil with nutrients.

Lupins are available in very many different shades of color: from white, yellow, orange, red, and pink to blue and purple. There are also bi-colored flowers. If the stalks are cut back completely after the first flush of flowers, the plant will send out more shoots and have a second, albeit weaker, flush in late summer.

A few Lupin varieties particularly useful for rock gardens are the carmine-red "Edelknabe"; "Kastellan" with white and dark-blue flowers; "Kronleuchter" with yellow flowers; and "Schlossfrau" with white and pink flowers.

Luzula nivea

Snowy Woodrush

20–60 cm

VI-VIII

This pretty grass grows naturally from northeastern Spain and central France to Slovenia and central Italy. It grows in light mountain forests and loves a moist, but well-drained, humus-rich, loamy soil. It forms a loose tussock of evergreen leaves with very attractive, thick clusters of white flowers that give the plant its name.

Snowy Woodrush is an excellent, fresh green ornamental grass for the rock garden. It is well suited as ground cover for partially shaded to shady areas and even tolerates the root pressure of larger trees. The leaves, which have hairy margins, grow to about 10–12 in (25–30 cm) long. Flower stalks of up to 24 in (60 cm) form from June through August with 6–20 whitish, tufted flowers arranged in dense clusters on each stalk.

Luzula nivea is a very undemanding, long-lived ornamental grass for the rock garden. This attractive plant is particularly well suited for underplanting trees and shrubs, but is also appropriate for heather gardens. In combination with Hostas and other shade-loving plants, it produces a rich and varied effect.

Lychnis

CAMPION

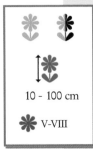

10 - 100 cm

V-VIII

Lychnis, also called Campion, is a long-lived, perennial plant. There are a lot of different species of *Lychnis*, the smaller ones being especially well suited to the rock garden. *Lychnis alpina* and *Lychnis coronaria* are particularly attractive.

■ LYCHNIS ALPINA: this species, also known as Alpine Campion, occurs naturally on scree and thin grassland in northern Europe and the Alps, the Apennines, and the Pyrenees. The basal leaves of the plant are arranged in a bushy rosette from which the upright flower stalks arise. The purple-red flowers, which appear between May and July, form impressive, almost spherical heads. This compact, evergreen perennial grows to a height of about 4–6 in (10–15 cm).

It thrives in a sunny to partially shaded place in moist, but well-drained, humus-rich soil that is low in lime and not too rich in nutrients. In the rock garden it is particularly effective in rocky cracks and crevices. In larger areas it will form mats over time.

■ LYCHNIS CORONARIA (photo): this species is also known as Rose Campion, Mullein Pink, and Dusty Miller. Growing to a height of 32–40 in (80–100 cm), this plant is rather better suited for larger rock gardens. It has silver-gray, hairy, felty leaves. Its magenta to carmine-red flowers, appearing between July and August, provide interesting splashes of color. Some varieties, such as "Alba", have white flowers. Rose Campion prefers a sunny to partially shaded position. The soil should be dry, well drained, and relatively poor.

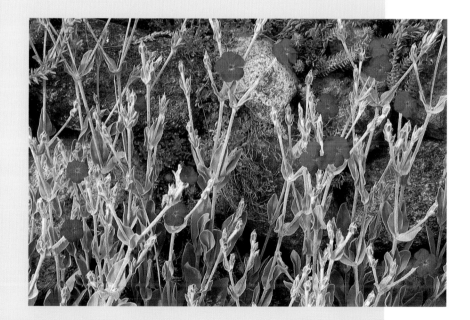

Lysimachia

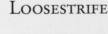

Loosestrife

5 - 80 cm

❋ V-VII

Loosestrife grows naturally on the banks of rivers and streams and in damp meadows. It comes originally from Europe, Japan, and North America. This pretty plant with its shiny, penny-shaped leaves is excellent for concealing edges.

This robust member of the Primrose family (*Primulaceae*) can also be used as ground cover in partial shade; it covers large areas very quickly. In view of its exuberant growth, however, it is advisable to keep it away from valuable Alpine plants.

Lysimachia nummularia, also known as Creeping Jenny (right), is an undemanding plant that forms beautiful cushions with its small, round leaves. The yellow, cup-shaped flowers appear from May through July. It requires moist soil to do well over a long period. One well-known variety is "Aurea", which is particularly attractive for its golden-yellow foliage and can also tolerate full sunlight. Another popular species of *Lysimachia* is the exquisite, yellow-flowered *Lysimachia punctata*, or Yellow Loosestrife. This perennial is an indestructible, long-lasting bloomer (June through August) with very vigorous growth, reaching a height of 32 in (80 cm).

Magnolia stellata

Star Magnolia

200 - 300 cm

III-IV

Magnolia stellata, also known as Star Magnolia for the star-like arrangement of its petals, flowers as early as March/April and, along with other early bloomers, heralds the spring in the rock garden.

This densely branched, bushy shrub has narrowly ovate to broadly lanceolate, dark- to light-green leaves. The white flowers, at times flushed with pink, appear before the leaves and clothe the shrub in a sumptuous, fragrant gown.

With a height of about 80–120 in (200–300 cm), Star Magnolia is a relatively small and dainty species of Magnolia and thus particularly well suited for the rock garden. The plant prefers a position with wind protection in sun or partial shade. The soil should be rich in nutrients and well drained, but moist. If necessary the early flowers of the Star Magnolia should be protected from late frosts.

Well-known varieties are "Royal Star" with double flowers; "Waterlily" with slightly larger flowers and pink-tinged buds; and "Rubra" with pinkish-purple flowers.

Melica ciliata

HAIRY OR SILKY MELIC

20 - 70 cm

V-VI

This plant, also known as Hairy or Silky Melic, is native to southern, central, and southeastern Europe, North Africa, and the Caucasus. It is found on sunny mountain slopes and on rocks on calcareous subsoil. In the rock garden it should be given a position as similar as possible to its natural habitat. This very attractive grass is often paid too little attention, but it is a pretty addition to stone beds.

Silky Melic forms upright clumps and reaches the considerable height of 8–28 in (20–70 cm). This makes it rather more suitable for slightly larger rock gardens. This deciduous plant has fine, gray-green leaves. The dense, slightly pendulous panicles of pearly, pale-green to light-brown flowers appear between May and June. As the seeds ripen the seed head turns a yellowish color, prolonging the ornamental value of the grass.

Melica ciliata grows well in a sunny spot and prefers calcareous, well-drained, sandy, and humus-rich soil. It is important that neighboring plants are prevented from crowding it.

Mesembryanthemum

Ice Plant

5 - 15 cm

❋ VII-IX

This plant comes originally from South Africa. It did not reach Europe and America until the 18th century and arrived on the Canary Islands in the 19th century. In the meantime it was also introduced into South Australia and the coasts of Japan.

In keeping with its origins, the Ice Plant should be given a dry, sunny position in the rock garden. This annual or frost-sensitive perennial is a beautiful, late summer bloomer: from July through September it is strewn with a profusion of daisy-like, white to reddish flowers. The plants make charming gap fillers.

Despite their name, most species of Ice Plant are not winter-hardy; neither are they long-lived. They should therefore be grown from seed as an annual, or over-wintered as cuttings of perennial species.

One orange species is *Mesembryanthemum putarielli*. Incidentally, the Ice Plant is also frequently referred to by the botanical name *Delosperma*. One species that can be recommended for its winter hardiness is *Delosperma nubigena*. It forms large, emerald-wgreen cushions dotted with numerous yellow flowers with reddish stamens.

SPECIALIST IN WATER CONSERVATION

Mesembryanthemum (mesembria is Greek for "midday") grows in the hot sun of South Africa. So as not to die of thirst, it has come up with a special technique: it holds its breath all day! Plants breathe through openings on the undersides of their leaves, through which they also lose water. So the Ice Plant closes these stomata, as they are called, during the day and only breathes after sunset. The carbon dioxide taken up during the night is then converted by photosynthesis into sugar and oxygen the next morning.

Muscari armeniacum

GRAPE HYACINTH

15 - 30 cm

✳ III-V

The Grape Hyacinth belongs to the Lily family (*Liliaceae*) and is a popular, undemanding bulb. These small, pretty plants flower between March and May and are welcome messengers of spring. Depending on species and variety, their color palette offers a broad spectrum of the most varied shades of blue. They are particularly suitable for mass planting in sunny rock gardens.

They prefer full sun, but will also tolerate partial shade. They grow especially well in well-drained, nutrient-rich soil. Besides *Muscari aucheri*, *Muscari botryoides*, and *Muscari comocum*, *Muscari armeniacum*, also known as the Armenian Grape Hyacinth, is a widely available species well suited to the rock garden. It comes originally from Armenia, the Caucasus, Asia Minor, Romania, and Macedonia. It grows to a height of about 6–12 in (15–30 cm) and bears its bright, cobalt-blue flowers with narrow white rims between March and May. *Muscari armeniacum* "Blue Spike" is a popular species that has sky-blue, double flowers.

Myosotis alpestris

ALPINE FORGET-ME-NOT

5 - 15 cm

✳ V-IX

The Alpine Forget-me-not is a short-lived, mostly biennial plant. It is worth sowing this attractive plant every year, however, so that you can always enjoy its pretty flowers. As the name suggests, the plant occurs naturally in the Alps, and also in pastures and rocky places in the mountains of Asia and North America.

This dainty plant only reaches a height of about 2–6 in (5–15 cm). Its narrow, slightly pointed, hairy leaves are green or brownish and very bushy, making the plant appear very compact. The flat, sky-blue flowers are borne in short, dense spikes and have a tiny, yellow eye in the centre. They appear from May through September.

The Alpine Forget-me-not is a great asset for the shadier parts of the rock garden. It grows particularly well in moist, but well-drained, soil that should also be rich in lime and nutrients. Otherwise, it is relatively easy to grow. Planted in small groups around rocks and by walls the fascinating blue flowers of *Myosotis alpestris* create beautiful accents. It goes well with Aquilegia, Campanula, and Clematis.

Narcissus

10 - 45 cm

III-V

Narcissus and Daffodil

Along with other early-flowering bulbs, Narcissi and Daffodils are cheerful messengers of spring in our gardens, with their beautiful colors and intoxicating fragrance. The beautiful youth, Narcissus, who fell in love with his own reflection and was later turned into a flower, gave his name to this enchanting plant. Nowadays there is a vast assortment of different Narcissus species to choose from and it is purely a matter of personal taste which ones you plant in your rock garden.

Depending on species and variety, Narcissi grow to a height of 4–18 in (10–45 cm). Their predominantly yellow, but sometimes also white or pink, flowers appear between March and May, with usually a single flower on each stem.

Depending on the size and structure of your rock garden, you can choose whether to have a show of large-flowered, garden Narcissi, or to fall back on the wild species, which are generally slightly smaller and fit in well with the overall scale of smaller rock gardens. There are also cultivated varieties that remain under 16 in (40 cm).

Narcissi prefer sunny to partially shaded positions in well-drained, nutrient-rich soil. It is important to remove the faded flowers so that they do not set seed. The leaves should be left until the plants have died back, however, as they are necessary for the intake and storage of nutrients.

Popular species

- NARCISSUS POETICUS (bottom): this species is also known as Poet's Narcissus, probably because its attractive flower and intoxicating perfume have inspired poets from time immemorial. The plant grows to a height of about 12–18 in (30–45 cm). The flowers, which appear from April through May, are creamy white. Well-known varieties include "Pheasant's Eye", whose flowers are white with a small, yellow, red-rimmed eye.

- NARCISSUS TRIANDUS (top): the smaller forms of this species, also known as Angel's Tears, which only grow to a height of 4–12 in (10–30 cm), are of special interest for the rock garden. The flowers are pale yellow to cream and several flowers are borne on each stem. Well-known varieties are the lemon-yellow "Hawera" and white-flowered "Thalia".

Nepeta

CATMINT

Nepeta is also known as Catmint because the plant attracts cats, which love to roll on it. The genus includes about 250 different species, native to the temperate regions of Europe, Asia, North Africa, and the mountains of tropical Africa.

The plant is mostly low growing and creeping, and has small, toothed, ovate to lanceolate leaves more or less covered in hair, which gives them a silvery- to gray-green appearance. Catmint is especially popular for its long flowering period. Between June and September the plant is covered in spikes of tiny, bilobed flowers in various shades of blue and purple, or white. Depending on species and variety, the plant can grow to a height of 10–32 in (25–80 cm; it exudes an aromatic, sometimes slightly lemony fragrance.

Nepeta loves full sun, but will also succeed in partial shade. The soil should be well drained. Cutting the plant back after flowering can stimulate a second flush of flowers. Catmint not only attracts cats, but it is also very attractive to butterflies and bees.

These perennial plants are very popular in the rock garden. In particular, the low-growing species are excellent for a variety of uses—as ground cover, for edging beds, and for dry-stone walls.

Examples of smaller species that are useful for the rock garden are *Nepeta faassenii*, with lavender blue flowers and a height of about 18 in (45 cm), and *Nepeta racemosa* with dark-violet through lilac-blue flowers and a height of 12 in (30 cm).

25 - 80 cm

VI-IX

Nothofagus antarctica

Antarctic or Southern Beech

The Antarctic or Southern Beech is native to the mountains of Chile. There, the tree can grow to a height of up to 100 ft (30 m); elsewhere, it only reaches a height of about 20–34 ft (6–10 m). It usually develops into a bush that, with its distinctive growth, makes an unusual, eye-catching feature.

Nothofagus antarctica frequently grows as a multi-stemmed shrub or tree, with the lower branches sometimes even lying on the ground. The branching structure is bizarre—the young twigs stand out from the branches quite regularly, like the bones of a fish.

Alongside this unusual growth, the small leaves with their crinkled edges and golden-yellow, fall tints are also attractive. By contrast the flowers, which appear in May, are rather insignificant, as are the fruits that ripen in fall. Another attractive feature of the Southern beech is its very beautiful, dark

6 -10 m

V-VI

brown bark with its distinctive light colored, horizontal stripes.

With its striking, filigree appearance, the Southern Beech is best used as a specimen tree. Its slow growth also makes it suitable for smaller to medium-sized gardens. The Southern Beech

also makes a good companion for other small leaved shrubs, such as Box, the Spindle tree, and Cotoneasters. Grasses such as Molina and Fountain Grass (*Pennisetum*) also make good neighbors.

The undemanding Southern Beech thrives in both sunny and partially shaded places. It prefers moist, but well-drained, soil that is lime-free and only moderately rich in nutrients. No pruning is needed.

Oenothera missouriensis

Evening Primrose

15 - 30 cm

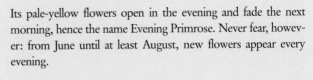 VI-IX

Its pale-yellow flowers open in the evening and fade the next morning, hence the name Evening Primrose. Never fear, however: from June until at least August, new flowers appear every evening.

Oenothera originally came from the dry steppes and hilly regions of North America; they first reached Europe as ornamental plants in the 17th century and, once there, quickly established themselves and spread. Today they are typically found on neglected sites such as railway embankments, landfill sites, and scree.

Oenothera missouriensis is the longest flowering of all the Evening Primrose species. This very vigorous, evergreen perennial can produce its cup-shaped, lemon-yellow flowers into September, and in this species the flowers are particularly large—up to five inches (13 cm) wide. On older plants, 30–40 flowers can be open at the same time.

This very undemanding plant prefers poor, gravelly, sandy or stony soil. It is therefore suitable for sunny slopes and scree beds. Because of its sprawling growth, Evening Primrose should be planted with space around it. It also presents an attractive picture when cascading from walls.

As it flowers over such a long period in the rock garden, *Oenothera missouriensis* needs lots of partners to set it off to best advantage all the time it is in bloom. Recommended companions are Campanula, Veronica, various species of Gentian, and Broom; it is also attractive in combination with blue-green grasses.

Papaver

Poppy

The name "Poppy" immediately brings to mind the exquisite, bright red splashes of color conjured up by the familiar Field Poppy in meadows and cornfields during the summer months. Most species in this varied genus first colonize arable land. Only a few have adapted to mountainous conditions, where they grow on rubble and scree. These species are naturally well suited to the rock garden.

The most important characteristic of this dainty plant is probably its shiny, silken flowers, which are reminiscent of crumpled paper. They appear singly on slim, hairy stems between May and July. The drooping buds give way to erect flowers when fully open, in glowing shades of red, pink, yellow, white, and orange, depending on species and variety. The leaves are blue-green, hairy, and pinnatifid. The plant grows to a height of 8–36 in (20–90 cm).

The plants grow best in full sun and moist, but well-drained, soil. In the rock garden, they are effective in scree, in walls, or among rocks. The smaller varieties especially are an attractive sight in troughs. The following two species are particularly well suited to rock gardens.

- PAPAVER NUDICAULE: this species, also known as the Iceland Poppy, is found in the Arctic and Subarctic regions of Asia and North America. It grows to a height of about 8–16 in (20–40 cm) and covers the whole color spectrum of the genus *Papaver* with its white, yellow, orange, pink, and red flowers that appear between April and September. The Iceland Poppy makes a very beautiful cut flower, if cut while still in bud. The variety "Gartenzwerg" is ideal for smaller rock gardens. This variety only grows to a height of 8–12 in (20–30 cm).

- PAPAVER ORIENTALE (left): this species is also called the Oriental Poppy. As the name suggests, the plant is native to the region of Asia Minor, Armenia, Northern Iran, and the Caucasus. The most striking feature of the Oriental Poppy is its impressive flowers, which in some varieties can be up to six inches (15 cm) across. It flowers between May and July. Here, too, the color spectrum ranges from white to shades of pink and orange to red. The plant can reach the considerable height of 20–36 in (50–90 cm). Smaller varieties such as "Pizzicato", which only grows to 20 in (50 cm), are more suitable for the rock garden.

20–90 cm

V-VII

Pennisetum

50 - 70 cm

VIII-IX

Fountain grass

Pennisetum, more particularly *Pennisetum alopecuroides*, is commonly called Fountain Grass, an apt name as the feathery flower heads are reminiscent of a fountain. The plant is native to Asia.

This grass, which forms dense, bushy clumps, has narrow, gray-green leaves. The tiny light- to reddish-brown flowers appear between July and September in fluffy plumes 6–10 in (15–25 cm) long. This evergreen plant has the added bonus that its decorative seed heads last well into the winter. Overall, this attractive plant reaches a height of 20–28 in (50–70 cm).

Pennisetum alopecuroides prefers full sun. The soil should be moist, but well drained, and rich in nutrients. Beautiful effects can be achieved in the late-summer rock garden with this magnificent ornamental grass. It is excellent either as a specimen plant or when planted in a group; it is happy among rocks, near water, or in beds and borders and can also be used as a tub plant. One very popular variety is the free-flowering "Hameln".

Phlox subulata

Moss Phlox

10 - 15 cm

IV-V

Phlox is a genus with many species of reliably flowering plants, ultimately all suitable for the rock garden. As the name Moss Phlox suggests, *Phlox subulata* forms dense, flat cushions about 4–6 in (10–15 cm) high. It spreads by means of rooting shoots.

Moss Phlox has needle-like leaves that grow densely on branching shoots. During the flowering period of April through May, the attractive appearance of this evergreen plant is crowned by a sumptuous mass of small flowers. Depending on variety, these can be round, longish, notched, or star-shaped, with a color palette ranging from white through violet, lavender blue, and pink to shades of blue, red, and purple.

Moss Phlox prefers a sunny spot and thrives in crevices and fine scree. The soil should be moist to moderately dry, nutrient-rich, and well drained. This plant is a typical, cushion-forming, rock garden plant. It is indispensable as ground cover, on dry-stone walls, and in rocky crevices. It is also very effective for edging beds and paths.

Phlox subulata is available in a great number of varieties, mainly differing in flower color, but also in flower size and growth.

Popular varieties include the vigorous, pale-blue flowered "G. F. Wilson"; the bright-red, large-flowered "Scarlet Flame"; the pale-blue flowered "Emerald Cushion Blue"; the pink-and-white striped "Candy Stripes"; and the vigorous, pure-white "White Delight".

Phyllitis scolopendrium

HART'S TONGUE FERN

30 - 40 cm

Hart's Tongue Fern, sometimes simply called Hart's Tongue, is a species belonging to the Spleenwort family (*Aspleniaceae*). It is distributed across many regions of the Temperate Zone of the Northern Hemisphere. One peculiarity of Hart's Tongue Fern is that its fronds are entire and non-pinnate (i.e., undivided). This distinguishes it from all other European ferns, which mostly have simple to multiple pinnate fronds.

Ferns can be used to provide attractive accents in the rock garden. The evergreen Hart's Tongue is of particular interest for partially shaded to shady areas in the garden. The new fronds produced in late spring are a fresh, pale green, while the older fronds are darker green and leathery. This plant feels particularly comfortable in calcareous, humus-rich and consistently moist soils and, depending on variety, can reach a height of about 12–16 in (30–40 cm).

Well-known varieties are "Angustifolia", with intensely dark green fronds that are 1½ in (2.5–4 cm) wide and 16 in (40 cm) long; "Capitata", with crested fronds ten inches (25 cm) long; and "Crispa", with waved frond margins.

Picea

SPRUCE

Spruce is a genus of evergreen coniferous trees and shrubs within the Pine family (*Pinaceae*). It is native to the Alps, the Mittelgebirge region of Germany, the Carpathians, the Pyrenees, the Balkans, and Russia.

The genus contains various species, such as *Picea glauca* (White or Canadian Spruce) and *Picea mariana* (Black Spruce). The best-known species, however, is undoubtedly the Norway Spruce (*Picea abies*) that has a reddish tinge to its bark.

The dwarf varieties of these species of Spruce, which grow to heights of 8–40 in (20– 100 cm), can be used to provide particularly attractive accents in the rock garden. Depending on species and variety, their growth is conical, spherical, spreading, cushion forming, or columnar. The plants are relatively robust and, like the larger species, can tolerate wind and low temperatures. They have stiff, sharply pointed needles that are mostly dark green in color.

Some popular varieties of *Picea abies* are "Compacta", a spherical, compact, and very dense variety; "Little Gem", with a flattened spherical shape; "Inversa", a very attractive Weeping Spruce (bottom); and Bird's Nest Spruce, "Nidiformis", with spreading growth and a flattened crown.

Popular varieties of *Picea glauca* are "Conica", the Dwarf Alberta Spruce with conical growth and dense, dark-green needles; and "Echiniformis" (left), with flattened spherical growth and blue-green, hoary needles.

20 - 100 cm

IV-VI

Pinus

Pine

The approximately 100 different species of Pine grow between the Arctic Circle and the Equator. *Pinus sylvestris*, the Scot's Pine, used to be called the "Fire Tree" or "Torch Tree" in Germany. Before the invention of electric light, chips of pinewood, which is particularly rich in resin, were cut and used as torches. Pine resin, also called turpentine or balsam, is an old medicinal remedy and the essential oil from pine needles is used as a bath oil.

Pine is one of the most unassuming trees, yet at the same time it belongs to one of the most beautiful and varied plant families. Pines require plenty of light and do not tolerate shade. They thrive on almost all soils, provided they are not too moist. New shoots, known as candles, are formed on the tips of the branches in May. Cutting these back will produce a beautiful, compact tree. While some species only have room in large gardens, other species and their many cultivated forms remain quite small and are thus well suited to the rock garden.

- PINUS MUGO: Mountain Pine. Numerous small-growing varieties and garden forms of Mountain Pine are available, e.g., *Pinus mugo* "Mops", a cushion-forming dwarf pine with flattened spherical growth. After 10–15 years, this plant will be 12–16 in (30–40 cm) high and 20–24 in (50–60 cm) across. Even smaller is the variety "Minimops", which is ideally suited to rock gardens of any size.

- PINUS MUGO MUGHUS: Mugho or Dwarf Mountain Pine. The Mugho Pine is accustomed to strong sunlight and freezing temperatures from its natural habitat in the Alps. It has compact, bushy growth and after five years will be about 20–24 in (50–60 cm) across and 16–20 in (40–50 cm) tall. With age, it can attain a height and spread of five feet (1.5 m).

- PINUS PARVIFLORA: Japanese White Pine. The most popular form of this species is *Pinus parviflora glauca*, a very attractive, slow-growing, multi-stemmed tree that reaches a height of 4–5 ft (1.2–1.5 m) in 10–15 years. The needles are bluish green to silvery blue and the cones are light brown.

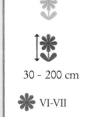

30 - 200 cm

VI-VII

- PINUS PUMILA: Dwarf Siberian Pine or Japanese Stone Pine. In this species, too, the *glauca* (blue) form is especially popular. With very robust branches and broad bushy growth, it grows to a height of about 40 in (1 m). Its intensely gray-blue needles are very striking.

Polypodium vulgare

POLYPODY

30 - 40 cm

When one thinks of ferns, sand dunes do not immediately spring to mind, but rather a wood with dappled shade or perhaps even the tropical forest. One fern, however, *Polypodium vulgare*, can commonly be seen growing on the dunes.

It is especially widely distributed in northern Germany, where it grows in acid soil in oak woods and in cracks in old sandstone walls. It also grows on the coast, where it is found on the shady northern and eastern slopes of the dunes. The sunny side does not suit it, as there it is in danger of drying out. That it can grow at all in open country without a protective canopy of trees is due to the high humidity of the sea air.

In contrast with most native ferns, which have greatly divided pinnate fronds, the fronds of Polypody are simple pinnate. In summer, double rows of spore capsules form on the undersides of the fronds, which turn brown as they mature in winter.

With its triangular, dark green, leathery fronds, *Polypodium vulgare* (*polypodium* means "many feet", in reference to its branched rhizomes) is an attractive fern for the rock garden. It

can be used to good advantage in the shadier areas, such as under trees. It is not a true ground-cover plant, but has tendencies in this direction. It is also well suited for growing in wall crevices. Polypody is evergreen if sufficient foliage surrounds it. The soil should be lime-free and the position partially shaded or shady. Suitable companion plants include Barrenwort, Foxglove, Solomon's Seal, and Bugbane.

Polystichum setiferum

Soft Shield Fern

40 - 75 cm

Ferns are probably among the oldest known plants. They are found growing wild in all parts of the world and in countless variations.

In the rock garden, ferns are indispensable for providing greenery in shady places and areas that receive no direct sunlight. They are often especially effective when in company with deciduous trees and conifers, or in rock and wall cracks.

Polystichum setiferum is also known as Soft Shield Fern and is probably one of the most elegant species of fern. It forms wide, funnel-shaped, bushy clumps and its stems are covered with scales and hairs.

One particularly attractive feature of this evergreen plant is its filigree fronds. These are multiple pinnate, matte green rather than glossy, and soft. The bushy plant grows to an average height of 16–30 in (40–75 cm).

The Soft Shield Fern prefers a partially shaded position, but will also tolerate brighter light provided it receives no direct sun and sufficient moisture is available.

Potentilla

Cinquefoil

Potentilla belongs to the Rose family (*Rosaceae*) and is a genus of many species. The smaller species are of special interest as rock garden plants.

The mat-forming or small bushy plants have green to silvery, hairy, digitate, or pinnate leaves. The flowers, which depending on species and variety appear between April and September, are relatively small, but their profusion and glowing colors more than compensate for their size.

In the rock garden, Cinquefoil thrives in full sun in scree, crevices, and walls. The soil should be well drained.

POPULAR SPECIES

- POTENTILLA ALBA: this species is also known as White Cinquefoil. It grows to a height of 5–10 in (12–25 cm) and bears white flowers from April to June.

- POTENTILLA AUREA: this plant bears yellow flowers between May and July and grows to a height of about 2–4 in (5–10 cm). One well-known variety is "Goldklumpen."

- POTENTILLA NEUMANNIANA: this species is also known as Spring Cinquefoil as it bears its yellow flowers from April onward. One particularly popular variety is "Nana," which only reaches a height of 1–2 in (3–5 cm).

- POTENTILLA NITIDA: this species is also known as Pink Cinquefoil. The plant grows to a height of 1½–3 in (2–8 cm) and bears pink flowers from July through September.

3 - 30 cm

IV-IX

Primula auricula

Primula

Alongside snowdrops and crocuses, Primulas are among the best-loved messengers of spring. After the gray of winter they provide cheerful splashes of color in every garden.

The genus *Primula* (roughly translated as "little firstling") includes more than 550 species and it is therefore difficult to do it justice. Without exception they are charming, delicate, predominantly rosette-forming plants. The flower stems, bearing tubular to saucer-shaped primrose flowers, either singly or in umbels, rise up from the middle of these rosettes.

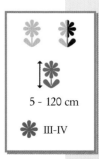

5 - 120 cm

III-IV

Popular species

PRIMULA AURICULA: this Alpine primula, also known simply as Auricula, is native to the high mountains where it grows in rocky crevices, on rubble, and in Alpine meadows. It likes calcareous, humus-rich, and stony soils, and is therefore well suited to a sunny or partially shaded position in the rock garden. It has yellow flowers from April through June and grows to a height of about four inches (10 cm).

PRIMULA DENTICULATA: this border species is also known as the Drumstick Primula. It prefers partial shade in any garden soil, and will only thrive in full sun if given a boggy soil. Varieties with pink, purple, or white flowers are available and they can reach a height of about eight inches (20 cm).

PRIMULA JAPONICA: this species, also known as the Japanese Primrose, is a Candelabra Primula, in which whorls of flowers are arranged in tiers around the long stems. This perennial plant requires a partially shaded to shady position in loamy, moist, but well-drained soil. Varieties in a range of colors are available from specialist nurseries.

PRIMULA VERIS: the yellow-flowered Cowslip, another Alpine Primula (*Vernalis* type), is a native meadow plant and undoubtedly one of the best-known species. It also should be assured a place in the rock garden. The Cowslip likes a partially shaded position in humus-rich soil.

In the rock garden, Primulas are generally suited for rocky crevices and fine scree. They go well with Saxifrage, Gentian, Pinks, and Campanula.

Prunus tenella

50 - 120 cm

IV-V

DWARF RUSSIAN ALMOND

Blossom trees were formerly too large for most rock gardens, but now there is an abundance of dwarf forms whose blossoms make a valuable contribution to the rock garden. One of these is *Prunus tenella*, the Dwarf Russian Almond. It is native to east-central Europe, central Asia, and eastern Siberia.

The plant forms a small, finely branched, bushy shrub and reaches a height of 20–48 in (50–120 cm). It is deciduous. Its green to brown branches are bare and shiny, turning more silvery gray in the second year. The leaves are one-inch (3 cm) long, serrate at the edges, and open between April and May.

The lovely, rose pink blossom appears at the same time, providing a truly splendid spectacle. The fruits of the plant are also very attractive. They develop from about August onward and beautify the rock garden in late summer and fall.

The plant prefers a sunny position and grows best in calcareous, humus-rich soil. The Dwarf Almond is especially effective in the rock garden when it can ramble between narrow rocky ledges. It produces suckers and is thus suitable for ground cover.

Pulsatilla vulgaris

Pasque Flower

Pulsatilla vulgaris, also known as the Pasque Flower, occurs naturally on dry grassland and heaths and on dry, calcareous slopes from England to the Ukraine. Its most important feature is its large, bell-shaped flowers, which have given rise to the botanical name—*pulsare* comes from the Latin and means "to strike" or "to ring". In the rock garden it is one of the most popular spring bloomers. Another very beautiful feature is the silky, silvery hairs that cover the buds, stems, and leaves, causing them to glisten attractively in the sun. The leaves are finely cut and dark green to gray-green in color. *Pulsatilla vulgaris* bears mostly purple, but also white, pink, or red, flowers, which open very early in spring, from March through May. The flowers are followed by feathery seed heads, which look like shaggy wigs and are also very attractive. The plant grows to a height of 6–12 in (15–30 cm).

The Pasque Flower grows best in a sunny, warm position, in poor, well-drained, calcareous soil, which should be moderately dry to moist. In the rock garden it is well suited to small niches, fine rubble, and scree. Suitable companion plants are Saxifrage, Primula, Gentian, and Campanula. It also creates an attractive picture with grasses, species of thyme, and *Adonis vernalis*. Caution is advised when dealing with the plant, since all its parts are poisonous and can cause skin irritation.

Well-known varieties of the Pasque Flower are the white-flowered "Alba", the wine-red-flowered "Rubra", the deep-red "Rote Glocke", and the pure-white "Weisser Schwan".

15 - 30 cm

III-V

Rhododendron

Rhododendron

It would be hard to imagine our parks and gardens without the *Rhododendron* genus and its massed profusion of flowering plants. Many people automatically associate Rhododendrons with England, where they grow into vast, wide bushes. That the shrub grows so luxuriantly on the island is due to the mild, misty, maritime climate. The real home of the Rhododendron, however, is Asia: Japan, Sumatra, Malaysia, and, above all, the Himalayas, where it covers whole ranges of hills in luxuriant forests.

The seeds of these wild species reached Europe almost 300 years ago. Since then the Rhododendron has swept away all before it in its triumphal march. Plant breeders experimented until they had made it winter-hardy for Northern Europe, and as an evergreen plant it is also attractive in the cold seasons of the year. The following are just a few of the vast number of Rhododendron species available. The ones described are also suitable for smaller rock gardens.

■ RHODODENDRON PRAECOX: this species leads
the dance of the Rhododendron flowers: in mild weather
it sometimes flowers as early as February; otherwise, its
clear rose-purple flowers appear from March through
April. An evergreen shrub, it has shiny, dark-green, oval
leaves with an aromatic fragrance. *Rhododendron praecox*
has loose, upright growth and reaches a height of about
4–5 ft (1.2–1.5 m). It is important to give it a sheltered
position—the plant itself is absolutely winter-hardy, but
the flowers are damaged by late frosts. After a frosty
night, the flowers will be mostly frozen or badly damaged. If there is a danger of late frost, therefore, the plants
should be protected with fleece.

120 - 150 cm

III-IV

Gardening tip

Rhododendrons require shady places and moist soil. In order to thrive, however, these plants must have an acid, i.e., lime-free, soil. Rhododendrons should be planted in holes about 12 in (30 cm) deep. The soil dug out of the planting hole should be mixed 1:1 with peat before being put back around the plant. The plants should be kept well watered.

■ RHODODENDRON HIRSUTUM: this profusely branched, rounded shrub only grows to 12–40 in (30–100 cm) and is densely covered in evergreen leaves. The leaves are fresh green and shiny above, with glandular scales on the underside. They are edged with bristly hairs. The many bell- or funnel-shaped flowers open in May/June. They are rose-purple, with white hairs inside, and grow in clusters of 3–10 flowers.

■ RHODODENDRON OBTUSUM JAPONICUM: Japanese Hybrid Azalea. As the name suggests, these hybrids come from Japan. They are deciduous shrubs, which are smaller growing than the evergreen Rhododendron species. They are mostly low, spreading, and dense and barely exceed 40 in (1 m) in height. The many different varieties bear a profusion of flowers in red, orange, pink, and white. These hybrids are particularly well suited for rock gardens, planted in a group in front of other Rhododendrons.

Robinia hispida

Rose Acacia or Bristly Locust

150 - 300 cm

V-VI

Robinia hispida is also known as Rose Acacia or Bristly Locust and occurs naturally in humid regions in southeastern North America, where the summers are hot.

Robinia is popular for its alternate, pinnate leaves and very attractive, pendent racemes of flowers. This large shrub has upright, sparsely branching growth and reaches a height of about 5–10 ft (1.5–3 m). Its pinnate leaves are dark green above and gray-green on the underside.

The branches are densely covered with red bristles. The exceptionally beautiful, light rose-pink flowers appear from May through June in hanging racemes, which in fall ripen to equally attractive, bristly, brown seedpods.

The plant grows best in full sun. It is relatively undemanding with regard to soil. It thrives in moist, but well-drained soil, yet will also cope with poor and rather dry soils. *Robinia* has very brittle branches and should be planted in the most wind-sheltered place possible. One very popular variety of Rose Acacia is "Macrophylla", or Large-Leaved Rose Acacia.

Rosmarinus officinalis

Rosemary

15 - 150 cm

III-VI

Rosmarinus officinalis, or simply Rosemary, is probably one of the best-known culinary herbs and there can hardly be a herb garden in which it does not grow. Mediterranean cuisine, in particular, would be difficult to imagine without this aromatic seasoning. In addition, Rosemary is said to have a beneficial effect on digestive complaints, rheumatic ailments, and circulatory problems. The plant is native to the Mediterranean region where it is found in rocky places, woods, underbrush, and thickets.

This slow-growing, evergreen shrub is not only popular for the aromatic flavor of its narrow, needle-like, blue-green leaves. The pale- to violet-blue, labiate flowers that appear between March and June are also very attractive.

The whole plant exudes a pleasantly aromatic fragrance, especially on warm, sunny days. Depending on variety, it can reach a height of 6–60 in (15–150 cm).

Rosemary grows best in a light position in full sun and well-drained soil. The small, low-growing varieties of *Rosmarinus officinalis*, in particular, are ideal plants for the rock garden. One good example is the blue-flowered "Prostratus", which only grows to six inches (15 cm).

Rudbeckia

70 cm

VII-IX

CONEFLOWER

The main decorative value of *Rudbeckia*, also called Coneflower, lies in its attractive, cheerful, yellow flowers. They seem to reflect directly the summer sun in the garden. This plant, originally from North America, is robust and relatively undemanding, which makes it a popular plant for the rock garden.

One especially beautiful variety is *Rudbeckia fulgida sullivantii* "Goldsturm", which at 28 in (70 cm) remains relatively small. This plant has either branching or unbranching stems with narrow, ovate-lanceolate, dark-green leaves, providing a pleasing contrast to the large, showy flowers. These are yellow with a dark center and appear in profusion between July and September.

The Coneflower loves a sunny position and nutrient-rich, moist, but well-drained, soil. In the rock garden its striking yellow flowers make a valuable addition to the plant collection.

Since they appear relatively late, they extend the flowering interest into the late summer and early fall when many other plants are already over. Planted in small or large groups, the plant is well suited for both beds and borders. It also makes a good cut flower.

Salix lanata

Woolly Willow

100 cm

III-IV

Willows are very diverse trees and shrubs and the various species can be used in many ways in the garden. They are popular for their shape, foliage, and (usually) very attractive catkins. With a height of 40 in (1 m), *Salix lanata*, also known as Woolly Willow, is one of the dwarf willows. It occurs naturally in damp meadows, by watercourses, and in gravelly soils from the high mountains of southern Scandinavia to the north of the Arctic Circle and northern Asia.

This compact, rounded, bushy shrub has thick boughs branching in all directions. The young shoots and winter buds have a dense, white, woolly covering, accounting for the plant's name. The young leaves also are covered in long, thick, white hairs, which they later lose to become dull green above and bluish green on the underside.

The long, elliptical, golden-yellow to yellow-gray catkins appear between March and April, before the leaves have opened. They make the Woolly Willow a very attractive ornamental plant for the rock garden. *Salix lanata* prefers a place in the sun and moist to moderately dry, well-drained soil.

Salvia nemorosa

SAGE

30 - 50 cm

VI-IX

Sage is undoubtedly best known as a culinary and medicinal plant, and has been used as a medication since Antiquity. This also explains its botanical name, which is derived from the Latin word *salvare*, meaning "to cure" or "to save." This plant occurs worldwide in temperate and tropical latitudes. It is found in sunny spots in dry meadows, on rocky slopes, in light thickets, and in moist grassland.

This sub-shrub has lanceolate, green to silver-gray leaves, which can be hairy to a greater or lesser extent. The color palette of the flowers, appearing between June and September, ranges from blue to violet and pink to red and white.

Sage prefers a dry, light, well-drained soil and sheltered position in full sun.

- SALVIA NEMOROSA: the blue to violet flower spikes of this species, also known as Woodland Sage, provide attractive accents in the rock garden. The fresh green foliage has a pleasantly aromatic fragrance. The plant flowers between June and September and, depending on variety, the blossoms are violet, purple, pink, and even white. *Salvia nemorosa* reaches a height of up to 20 in (50 cm). Well-known varieties are the purplish-red "Lubecca", violet-flowered "Ostfriesland", and white-flowered "Schneehügel".

- SALVIA OFFICINALIS: this species, also known as Common or Garden Sage, is the traditional medicinal and culinary herb with aromatic leaves. The plant bears its lilac-colored flowers from June through August and grows to a height of about 18–20 in (45–50 cm). Popular varieties are the violet-flowered "Aurea" and "Purpurascens" and the blue-flowered "Tricolor".

Saponaria ocymoides

Rock Soapwort

This plant is called Soapwort because it contains saponin, a substance that foams like soap when dissolved in water. The botanical name is also derived from *sapo*, the Latin word for "soap." Soapwort was formerly used as a washing agent. In addition, it is reputed to have medicinal properties—it is said to liquefy phlegm in the bronchial passages and thereby to have a beneficial effect on diseases of the respiratory tract. It is also said to be helpful in combating skin rashes and eczema.

This plant occurs naturally on mountain slopes in southern and southeastern Europe, and its spreading growth makes it mainly suitable for larger rock gardens. With its mostly prostrate shoots, it forms extensive carpets about 4–8 in (10–20 cm) in height. The leaves are oblong to acicular. Soapwort is especially attractive in the summer months of June and July when the evergreen cushions are strewn with a profusion of small, pretty flowers in dense, crowded cymes. The color spec-

trum lies in the red or pink range, but there are also white-flowered varieties.

Saponaria ocymoides is one of the popular, more undemanding rock garden plants. It prefers a sunny position and moist, but
well-drained, calcareous soil. In the rock garden it will thrive in
rocky crevices and scree. It can be used to provide greenery on
scree beds and slopes and thus stabilize loose subsoil. These
bright, attractive cushions are also suitable for beautifying dry-
stone walls. Well-known varieties are the white-flowered "Alba",
compact, dark-red "Rubra Compacta", and intensely rose-pink
"Splendens".

10 - 20 cm

VI-VII

Saxifraga

Saxifrage

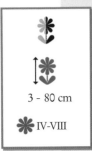

3 - 80 cm

✳ IV-VIII

With its unbelievable diversity of species and varieties, the genus *Saxifraga*, also known as Saxifrage, contains some of the most important plants in the rock garden. Below we describe a few species from the infinite variety of Saxifrage plants.

■ SAXIFRAGA COTYLEDON (right): this species is also known as Maiden Saxifrage. It is native to central Europe, Scandinavia, Iceland, and North America, and has striking, 6–32 in (15–80 cm), many-branched flower sprays. Also of particular interest are its lime-encrusted rosettes of glistening, tongue-shaped, silvery leaves. The flowers, which are mostly white, but sometimes also yellow, appear between June and August. The plant feels most comfortable out of direct sunlight, but under certain circumstances can also tolerate full sun. The soil should be moist, but well drained, and contain some lime. In the rock garden this species is well suited to rocky crevices, wall cracks, and stony slopes. Well-known varieties are "Caterhamensis" (white flowers with red spots) and the white-flowered "Pyramidalis".

■ SAXIFRAGA DACTYLOIDES (LEFT): this group includes the mossy Saxifrage species. They form carpets of countless rosettes of soft, green leaves that cover the ground like a blanket of fur. Well-known species within this group are the *Arendsii* hybrids, *Saxifraga muscoides* and *Saxifraga trifurcata*. The various species bear their white, pink, red, or yellow flowers between April and June. The plants grow to a height of 2–10 in (5–25 cm). All species prefer cool spots, out of direct sunlight or in partial shade, and well-drained, humus-rich soils. They are well suited for planting on slopes, in rocky niches and walls, and also between larger rocks. Well-known varieties of *Arendsii* hybrids include "Rosenzwerg", with dark pink flowers; the dark-red "Triumph"; and the white-flowered "Grandiflora Alba".

■ SAXIFRAGA MOSCHATA: this species is also known as Mossy or Musky Saxifrage. It grows to a height of about 1–4 in (3–10 cm) and smells strongly of resin. *Saxifraga moschata* flowers from July through August.

Scilla

SQUILL

The blue, star-shaped flowers of *Scilla* are an eye-catching sight, bringing a cheerful breath of spring to the garden. They are easy to grow and almost indestructible, properties that make them especially valuable for the rock garden.

These plants grow best in a sunny to partially shaded position, although some species will also grow in light shade. The soil should be moist, but well drained, and rich in humus. Like all small bulbs in the rock garden, they are best planted in groups. A few specimens are also suitable for troughs. Those species that increase freely should be placed at the edge of flowerbeds or woodland.

15 - 30 cm

III-V

POPULAR SPECIES

- SCILLA HISPANICA (right): this species, native to Spain and Portugal, is also known as the Spanish Squill or Spanish Bluebell, because of the small, bell-shaped flowers that grow in pyramid-shaped clusters on its robust stems. The plant usually has blue flowers, but there are also lilac, pink, and white varieties. It flowers between April and May. Outwardly, *Scilla hispanica* looks a little like a hyacinth and it is sometimes also known as *Hyacinthoides hispanica*. It grows to a height of 8–12 in (20–30 cm).

- SCILLA SIBIRICA (left): this species is distributed from Russia to the Caucasus and Asia Minor and is also known as Siberian Squill. The bright blue, star-shaped flowers are borne on approximately six inch (15 cm) stems between March and April. It is very vigorous and can self-seed to cover large areas of a rock garden. There are, however, varieties in which this problem does not arise, as they only increase by offsets. "Spring Beauty" is one such variety.

Sedum

STONECROP

Like Saxifrage, the genus *Sedum*, commonly known as Stonecrop, contains an almost unimaginable diversity of species and varieties.

Almost all of these nigh-on indestructible plants can succeed in relatively inhospitable conditions. For instance, they tolerate very arid conditions by storing water in their fleshy leaves. These plants are not only popular because they are so easy to grow, however—they are also very attractive. They enhance the rock garden with their beautiful, often very colorful foliage and become a real feast for the eyes in summer when they are covered in countless small, star-shaped flowers in yellow, pink, red, or white.

All species are relatively undemanding. They prefer a sunny, warm position, but can also tolerate partial shade. The plants thrive in dry scree and in crevices, and the soil should be well drained. They are particularly well suited to the rock garden, where they can be used in a multitude of ways: on slopes, on the tops of wall, in cracks between paving slabs, and along paths. These carpet-forming plants can even serve as a kind of lawn substitute in very dry places or other areas where a lawn cannot be grown. Some species can be used for ground cover. The smaller species are also extremely effective in troughs. Three examples of popular species are described in more detail below.

POPULAR SPECIES

■ SEDUM ACRE: this evergreen perennial, also known as Wall Pepper or Biting Stonecrop, gets its name from its hot-tasting leaves. It forms carpets about two inches (5 cm) in height and has pale-green leaves. Its star-shaped flowers are bright yellow and appear from June through July. In general, care is needed with this species, as it can be very invasive and become a weed.

■ SEDUM FLORIFERUM: this species is also known as Kamschatka or Russian Stonecrop. It forms dense mats

5 - 20 cm

❋ VI-IX

that closely hug the ground, growing to a height of about 4–8 in (10–20 cm). The dark-green leaves are winter-hardy and can acquire attractive purple fall tints. The yellow flowers appear between July and September.

SEDUM SPURIUM: this species, also known as Two-Row Stonecrop, is exceptionally striking with its umbrella-shaped, pink to red flowers. The plant blooms between June and August and grows to a height of about 4–8 in (10–20 cm).

Sempervivum

Houseleek

Like almost all representatives of the *Crassulaceae* family, the evergreen Houseleek, also known as Roof Houseleek, is a succulent, meaning that it can store water in its leaves. It occurs predominantly in the Mediterranean region from Morocco to Iran, mainly in barren, dry places with little precipitation. It also grows in rocky places, in wall cracks, and in the mountains to an altitude of 9,000 ft (2,800 m).

The name *Sempervivum* comes from the Latin—translated literally, it means "ever living", which refers not only to the plant's long lifespan, but also its frugality and toughness, often growing under difficult conditions.

For the Houseleek fan, the attraction of the many different species and their countless varieties lies in their spherical rosettes of fleshy leaves in the most varied colors and shapes. This foliage, which serves as a water reservoir, ensures that the plants can survive even protracted dry spells with no ill effects. The flower stem, which is covered in leaves overlapping like roof tiles, grows out of the rosette. The

star-shaped flowers are borne in cymes and are red, yellow and, more rarely, white. After flowering the rosette dies, but it will already have formed several offsets. In this way the Houseleek covers smallish areas with rosettes of different sizes.

One species often used in the rock garden is the Common Houseleek (*Sempervivum tectorum*). It is remarkably variable in rosette size and coloring. The flat, open rosettes can be small with a diameter of 2–3 in (5–7 cm), but there are also types with rosettes up to 8 in (20 cm) across.

The very fleshy leaves are green, often reddish in dry conditions, with a clear, brown, pointed tip. The flowers of the Common Houseleek are mostly purplish rose.

5 - 40 cm

VI-VIII

With their attractive rosettes, Houseleeks are ideal, undemanding rock garden plants. They thrive in rocky crevices, stone cracks, and on the tops of walls. The colors of the rosettes should contrast with the stones in the rock garden—green and gray rosettes with red sandstones; rosettes in shades of red with yellowish and gray limestones.

One point to note is that the plants require a sunny position and well-drained soil, as they cannot tolerate wet conditions. They go well with Campanula, Crane's Bill, Saxifrage, and Outdoor Cacti, as well as Gentian, Yucca, and Creeping Thyme.

Stachys

WOUNDWORT

Stachys lanata (left), also known as *Stachys byzantina*, Lamb's Ears, Woundwort, and Woolly Betony, is distributed from the Caucasus to northern Persia. It grows naturally on dry, rocky hillsides, in scrub, pastureland, and woodland clearings, and on riverbanks. This mat-forming perennial has rosettes of thick, gray-green leaves densely covered in white, woolly hairs. The flower stalks are also covered in white, woolly hairs and bear small, pinkish-purple flowers arranged in whirls from June through August. Lamb's Ears grow to a height of about 6–20 in (15–50 cm).

Stachys lanata grows best in hot, dry places in full sun. The soil should be well drained and moderately fertile. If you prefer the silvery-gray cushions of foliage without the flower stalks, you can simply cut them off. In the rock garden, this plant is especially suitable for ground cover or edging.

Well-known varieties include the sparsely flowering "Silver Carpet" with gray-white leaves flushed with silver and "Cotton Boll" with globular, cottony flowers. *Stachys grandiflora* "Superba" (bottom) is a particularly beautiful variety.

15 - 50 cm

VI-VIII

Stipa

FEATHER GRASS

50 - 80 cm

VI-VIII

Stipa, also called Feather Grass, occurs in the temperate to tropical dry regions of the earth. It is especially prized for its wheat-like flower plumes with arching feathery awns up to 16 in (40 cm) long. They shimmer like silvery silk and stir in the slightest breath of wind like feathers, thus living up to their name. The clumps of narrow, gray-green leaves are also extremely pleasing, growing to a height of about 32 in (80 cm).

The plant prefers a warm, sunny position in dry, calcareous, well-drained soil. It is relatively easy to grow, but sensitive to winter wet.

The graceful, slender flower stems playing lightly in the wind bring a touch of artistry to the rock garden. Beautiful effects can be achieved by planting Feather Grass in groups, and it is particularly effective when planted next to blue-flowered Sage or Veronica. The seed heads are also very attractive in bouquets.

Tagetes

Marigold

15 - 120 cm

V-X

The irrepressible Marigold surely needs no introduction, as the plant is very well known and popular. It owes its popularity to its immense capacity for flowering, uncomplicated care, and diversity of form, which makes its so versatile.

The genus *Tagetes* includes about 50 species of strongly scented, bushy annuals and perennials, coming originally from Mexico and Central America. They are divided into three hybrid groups:

— TAGETES ERECTA: this group, known as African Marigolds, has compact growth and very large, fully double, globular flowers held well above the foliage on sturdy stems. There are varieties of up to four feet (1.2 m) in height, such as "American", which is available with both yellow and orange flowers, and also smaller varieties such as "Discovery", which only grows to 6–10 in (15–25 cm) and also has yellow or orange flowers. "Goldschmied", "Jubilee", "Smiles", and "Sovereign" grow to 20–28 in (50–70 cm) and also flower in variations of yellow and orange.

■ TAGETES PATULA: this group, also known as French Marigolds, have slightly smaller flowers similar to carnations, and are generally not so tall—ranging from "Boy" at only about 8 in (20 cm), through "Disco Orange" (10–12 in/ /25–30 cm) to "Tangerine" (12–16 in/30–40 cm).

■ TAGETES TENUIFOLIA: this group, also known as Signet or Lemon Marigolds, is the daintiest representative of the genus with small, star-shaped flowers among finely divided foliage. Reliable varieties are the orange-flowered "Carina" (10 in/25 cm); the golden-yellow "Gnom" (12 in/ 30 cm); the pale-yellow "Lulu" (12 in/30 cm); the red-brown "Ornament" (8–10 in/20–25 cm); and the golden-yellow "Ursula" (12 in/30 cm).

Tagetes combines especially well with blue-flowered partners such as ornamental Sage and Heliotrope, and also Calendula, Lobularia, and Chrysanthemums.

Taxus baccata

Yew

The Yew (*Taxus*) belongs to the Yew family (*Taxaceae*). These evergreen bushes and trees are very slow-growing and can attain a great age.

The best-known species of Yew is probably *Taxus baccata*, the Common or English Yew. This poisonous plant has thin, gray to red-brown, scaly bark. The needles are dark green above and light green on the underside. The flowering period is March through April. The different varieties can grow to a height of about 33–60 ft (10–18 m). Dwarf varieties, on the other hand, remain quite small—about 20–40 in (50–100 cm). The cushion and columnar forms are especially suitable for the rock garden, only growing to a few feet in height.

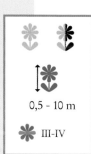

0,5 - 10 m

III-IV

Taxus baccata prefers a sunny to partially shaded spot in moist, but well-drained soil that is not too acid. It is not so well suited to windy positions.

One particularly well-known and popular variety of *Taxus baccata* is "Fastigiata", also known as the Irish Yew.

Like all Yew species, it grows rather slowly, reaching a height of about five feet (1.5 m) in ten years. Its most attractive features are its erect, upright growth, reminiscent of a slender pillar, and its red fruits. Other interesting varieties for the rock garden are "Repandens", the Spreading English Yew, and *Taxus cuspidata* or, "Nana", the Dwarf Japanese Yew.

Thymus

THYME

Thyme is almost certainly known to everyone as a culinary herb used for flavoring or as a cough remedy. With its wonderful fragrance and extremely attractive appearance, however, it should not be left out of any rock garden.

The evergreen perennial herbaceous plants, shrubs, and sub-shrubs of this genus mainly form prostrate carpets about 2–6 in (5–15 cm) high, which can become relatively large over time. The leaves are oval to acicular, hairy, and have an aromatic fragrance and taste. Between June and October small red, pink, violet, or white flowers appear above the dense foliage.

Thyme prefers a warm, sunny position and thrives in Alpine meadows and fine rubble. The soil should be well drained. If the carpets become too large, you can simply cut them

back. It is also best to cut back vigorous species of Thyme to keep the growth compact.

In the rock garden, Thyme makes itself at home in fine scree or in crevices. It is also suitable for dry-stone walls. Smaller species can be used for troughs. Two examples of Thyme species are:

5 - 30 cm

VI-X

THYMUS SERPYLLUM (top): this mat-forming sub-shrub is also known as Wild Thyme. It grows to a height of about 2–4 in (5–10 cm) and flowers between June and October. Well-known varieties are "Albus" (2 in/5 cm) with white flowers and "Coccineus" (2 in/5 cm) with scarlet flowers.

THYMUS VULGARIS (left): this bushy, cushion-forming sub-shrub, also known as Common or Garden Thyme, is mainly used as a culinary herb. It grows to a height of about 12 in (30 cm) and flowers from May through September.

Tsuga canadensis

Eastern or Canadian Hemlock

70 - 100 cm

The wild form of *Tsuga canadensis*, also called Eastern or Canadian Hemlock, often grows in marshy terrain in its North American home. The attractive dwarf-growing varieties are suitable for the rock garden where, in keeping with their natural habitat, they should be planted in cool, moist places.

Tsuga canadensis can be recognized by its arching branches with their soft, flat, dark-green needles. These are around two-fifths of an inch (1 cm) long and have white lines on the underside.

Eastern Hemlock prefer a partially shaded position, but can also grow in full sun. In either case, the soil should be cool, moist, and well drained.

One of the best-known and most popular varieties for the rock garden is the Dwarf Hemlock *Tsuga canadensis Jeddeloh*. It has hemispherical, nest-like growth and long needles. The plant grows to a height of 28–40 in (70–100 cm). One particularly attractive and interesting feature of this variety is the spiraling arrangement of its branches.

Tulipa

Tulip

Originally from the temperate regions of Asia, these bulbs are among the best-known and best-loved ornamental plants. Since the "tulip mania" of the 17th century in Holland, when tulip bulbs changed hands for exorbitant prices, many people have considered tulips to be part of the Dutch stereotype. Dutch breeders indeed supply a large proportion of the tulips on the market today.

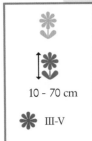

10 - 70 cm

III-V

Tulips are characterized by upright growth, reaching heights of 4–28 in (10–70 cm). The white, red, yellow, orange, pink, and bi-colored flowers appear between March and May. There is such a diversity of species, varieties, and hybrids that hardly a wish remains unfulfilled with regard to flower color and shape—there is a tulip to suit every taste. In general, however the stately, tall-stemmed garden tulips are less well suited to the rock garden, while the smaller, wild types with their varieties and hybrids fit in better, creating an exquisite picture in spring. The plants prefer a sunny position and nutrient-rich, well-drained soil. In the rock garden they are effective in smallish or larger groups: for example, among stones or small shrubs.

POPULAR SPECIES

- TULIPA GREIGII HYBRIDS (bottom): the *Greigii* hybrids are always crosses between Wild Tulips. Their leaves have dark marks or stripes and they grow to 6–12 in (15–30 cm). Their small height means that they are excellently suited for rock gardens. The large, mainly red or yellow flowers appear in early/mid spring.

- TULIPA TARDA: this Dwarf Tulip species comes originally from central Asia. It grows to a height of 4–6 in (10–15 cm) and has star-shaped, creamy-white flowers with a yellow center. Being very long-lived and a compact size, this plant is one of the most valuable species for the rock garden.

- TULIPA KAUFMANNIANA HYBRIDS (top): these plants, also known as Water Lily Tulips, are robust and relatively long-lived. They grow to a height of about 6–10 in (15–25 cm). The main colors are yellow, red, and white. These plants are especially popular for their early flowering period, in March and April.

Verbascum

MULLEIN

Verbascum or Mullein grows straight as a dart to the majestic height of 6–7 ft (2 m), with bright yellow flowers opening over much of its length, releasing a wonderful perfume and attracting butterflies and bees. It is also an important and well-known herbal remedy, particularly for a dry cough.

The plant is biennial. In the first year it forms a rosette of gray-green, velvet-soft leaves. In the second year a stem pushes up out of the rosette. It is unbranched or only slightly branched and bears the flowers, which open gradually—from bottom to top—from June through September. There are also species that flower again in the second or third summer, provided they have a sunny position and poor soil. These species are classed as short-lived perennials.

Mullein makes an excellent accent plant in the rock garden. With its evergreen rosette

HILDEGARD OF BINGEN AND MULLEIN

There is no warmer, more comforting yellow than that of Mullein flowers.
Eight hundred years ago, Saint Hildegard gave the following prescription to
people who had a sad heart: "Whoever has a weak and sad heart should
cook and eat Mullein with meat and fish or cake, then will his heart be
strengthened and be joyful again". Perhaps this recipe is connected with the
joyful, sunny color of the Mullein flowers.

20 - 200 cm

VI-IX

of leaves, it is also an extremely
attractive plant in winter, being very
robust and adaptable. In addition,
the choice of flower color is no
longer restricted to yellow. Plant
breeders have developed varieties
with red, white, pink, violet, and
salmon-color flowers. Growth habit
can also vary. Branched and straight
stems, dense and delicate flower
spikes, and differing heights offer
sufficient diversity to meet individual
requirements.

Popular species

- VERBASCUM OLYMPICUM (left): in this species, from June through August, individual yellow flowers are densely packed on a 6–7 ft- (2 m)-high flower spike, branched like a candelabra.

- VERBASCUM DUMULOSUM (page 283): this species differs markedly from the normal form of growth. It forms densely bushy sub-shrubs 8–12 in (20–30 cm) high, with lemon-yellow flowers. It is a very pretty, slightly frost-sensitive species.

- VERBASCUM SPECIOSUM: a very large (6–7 ft/2 m) Mullein with broad, velvety leaves covered in white hairs and moderately branched spikes of large, sulfur-yellow flowers.

- VERBASCUM PHOENICEUM: this species, growing to the modest height of 16–24 in (40–60 cm), can also be used in smaller rock gardens. The flower spikes and lower part of the stems are mostly red-violet in color, while the flowers themselves are violet-purple. There are also pink- and white-flowered types.

- VERBASCUM DENSIFLORUM: this species is distinguished by large, lemon-yellow flowers. It grows to a height of about 40 in (100 cm).

Verbena bonariensis

Brazilian Verbena

This impressive plant, also known as Brazilian Verbena, Purpletop Verbena, or Purpletop Vervain, has small, fully-double, globular flowers, which appear to float formally on the long, branching, almost leafless stems. This not quite winter-hardy perennial from Argentina (*bonariensis* = Buenos Aires = good air) has quite particular charm—its lavender-blue flowers bloom far into the autumn.

The Brazilian Verbena belongs to a genus of about 250 species, mainly occurring in the tropical and temperate latitudes of America. They usually colonize open, sunny habitats such as prairies, roadside verges, and light woodland.

One species native to Europe is Vervain, *Verbena officinalis*. One of its common names, Iron Weed, can be explained by the fact that it was formerly used to heal wounds caused by iron weapons.

80 - 140 cm

VII-X

With its very long flowering period, *Verbena bonariensis* makes a valuable contribution to the summer and fall garden. In spite of its height, the plant takes up little space, as its sparse foliage gives it a translucent and airy feel. It has a wonderfully enlivening effect in yellow borders: for example, with Coreopsis, Rudbeckia, and Helenium. It is, admittedly, rather tender and will only survive the winter in mild positions or with protection, but there are usually plenty of seedlings.

Veronica

SPEEDWELL

10 - 20 cm

V-VI

Veronica, also known as Speedwell, is enchanting, and not only for its extremely decorative, often silvery-gray foliage. The attractive racemes of (mostly) blue flowers also provide wonderful accents in the rock garden. In the wild the plant grows naturally in forest clearings, on sunny scree slopes, and among underbrush.

An example of a particularly charming species is *Veronica prostrata*, also known as Prostrate Speedwell, whose creeping shoots can form dense mats. Long-stemmed flower spikes in the form of densely packed conical clusters appear from May through June. The flowers are usually pale- to dark-blue, but there are also white- and pink-flowered varieties. Prostrate Speedwell grows to a height of about 4–8 in (10–20 cm).

The plant grows best in a sunny position and in well-drained, moist to moderately dry soil. In the rock garden it is suitable as ground cover or for planting in rocky crevices and cracks in dry-stone walls. It goes well with Campanulas, Rock Roses, and Lobularia. Well-known varieties are the white-flowered "Alba", the pink-flowered "Rosea", and "Pallida" with pale, china-blue flowers.

Viola

HYBRIDS

Violet or Pansy

The Violet is one of the best-known and best-loved flowers. It has been celebrated by countless poets and is probably only surpassed in popularity by the Rose. In folk medicine, too, the Violet has been prized for its healing powers since Antiquity.

The genus *Viola* (belonging to the *Violaceae* family) includes about 500 species of annuals, perennials, and sub-shrubs, found in temperate zones from the Subarctic to the mountains of New Zealand. *Viola* is also native to Europe and occurs in woods and grassland in the form of the Dog Violet (*Viola canina*).

The most striking feature of all species is the distinctive flowers, which consist of five segments and are borne on long stems. The predominant flower colors are violet, white, and yellow. The lower, middle petal often has a darker marking. The Violet and Pansy that we know as garden plants have been produced by hybridization.

On the following page, we describe two species of the large Violet family in more detail.

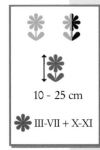

10 - 25 cm

III-VII + X-XI

■ VIOLA CORNUTA: this species, known as Horned Violet or Johnny Jump-Up, is a nonstop bloomer that can bring even the most insignificant corner of a garden to life. Its small, typical, violet flowers, growing to a height of 4–10 in (10–25 cm), rise up out of dark-green foliage. In the pure species they are blue-violet, but there are also countless hybrids featuring an array of colors. After its long flowering period (May through July) the Horned Violet can even flower again in October and November if cut back after the first flush. This also keeps the plant more compact. Small, bushy, and cushion forming, it is well suited to the rock garden and makes a particularly pleasing display with Lobularia, Arabis, Anemones, and Veronica.

■ VIOLA WITTROCKIANA: Garden Pansies are the most widespread spring bloomers. Their cheery, colorful flowers give pleasure from March onward. The *Viola wittrockiana* hybrids are the result of the hybridization of various species and are cultivated as annuals or biennials. There are varieties with small flowers similar to the Horned Violet, but also large-flowered varieties such as the well-known "Swiss Giants". Pansies form bushy, evergreen plants with heart-shaped green to dark-green leaves. The flowers, which can be 2½–4 in (6–10 cm) across, have overlapping petals. They are available in single colors (usually white, yellow, orange, pink, red, blue, or purple) and in two colors, with and without an eye. The plant prefers a sunny to partially shaded position and light, nutrient-rich soil. With their glowing colors, Pansies are an absolute eye-catcher in the rock garden. They combine well with Tulips, Hyacinths, and other spring flowers.

Wulfenia carinthiaca

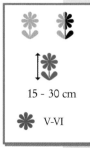

15 - 30 cm

❈ V-VI

Cow's Footsteps

Wulfenia carinthiaca probably owes its strange name, Cow's Footsteps, to its origins in mountain pastures and meadows in the southeastern Alps. This attractive, evergreen, rosette-forming plant has shiny, dark-green leaves. The abundant flower spikes appear from May through June. Usually the small, narrow, bell-shaped flowers are bluish violet, but there are also white varieties. The flowers are borne in a second (on one side only) cluster on the end of the stem. The plant grows to a height of about 6–12 in (15–30 cm).

Wulfenia should be given a sunny to semi-shady place with sufficient air humidity. It grows best in humus-rich, well-drained soil, which should be slightly acid. In addition, the plants cannot tolerate excessive wet, and should be protected against it.

In the rock garden, *Wulfenia carinthiaca* shows to particular advantage between rocks, in crevices, and in wall cracks. Suitable companions include Primulas, Prunella, and grasses.

One well-known variety is the white-flowered "Alba".

Yucca filamentosa

ADAM'S NEEDLE

75 - 150 cm

VII-VIII

Yuccas have enjoyed great popularity for many years. Although commonly called Yucca Palms, strictly speaking they are not true palms; botanically, they belong to the Agave family (*Agavaceae*). The genus includes about 40 species, which are native to the drier regions of North and Central America.

Yuccas are perennial plants, trees, and shrubs: some form trunks while others do not, with foliage arranged in rosettes, rather reminiscent of palms. The leaves are mostly hard to leathery, often toothed or with fibrous threads on the edges. Upright stalks bearing numerous cup-shaped, mostly white or cream flowers rise up out of the center of the rosette.

One species suitable for the rock garden is *Yucca filamentosa*. This almost trunkless shrub with its rosette at ground level makes a striking accent plant. It will not fit into tight corners of the garden, but is better suited for positions more like its natural habitat in the sparsely vegetated desert. Its dark-green leaves, up to 30 in (75 cm) long, have loose fibers on the edges. In midsummer, *Yucca filamentosa* sends out a flower stalk at least three feet in height, bearing bell-shaped, usually white flowers. This species is also frost-hardy in temperate latitudes and grows best in full sun with good drainage.

Yucca filamentosa is available in various colors and sizes. "Bright Edge" is a particularly attractive variety with a broad, yellow edge to its leaves. In "Variegata" the blue-green leaves have a white edge and are flushed with pink in winter. "Fontäne" grows to a height of four feet (1.2 m) and "Glockenriese" grows to about five feet (1.5 m). Yucca flowers are usually white; in the "Schneetanne" variety they have a slight yellowy-green tinge.

Index of common names